Holy Macro! Books
Books for Spreadsheet People in the Age of AI

PO Box 541731, Merritt Island FL 32954

ChatGPT for the Rest of Us

First Publication: August 5, 2026

Authors: Kim Sekas and Bill Jelen

Indexer: Nellie Jay

Compositor: Jill Cabot

Copy Editor: Jody Sekas

Cover Design: Mike Kass

Published by: Holy Macro! Books, PO Box 541731, Merritt Island FL 32954

Distributed by Independent Publishers Group, Chicago, IL

ISBN 978-1-61547-096-9 (print) 978-1-61547-183-6 (digital)

Version 202600906a

Table of Contents

Dedication

Kim: To the Prompt Monkeys

Bill: To the Morning Crew

Thanks to

Kim: The Prompt Monkeys (AI Adventurers): Angela Bernardo, Susan Hutt, Stacie Fuss, Bill Jelen, Connie Marceline, Michelle Hennis, Cyndi Moraitis, Alina Bankal, and Wendy Early. Jane Sekas (AI Absolutist). Jody Sekas (AI Agnostic). Chris Henning & Shannon Hazen (for Wifi and listening).

Bill: Suat Ozgur. Kim Sekas. Stacie Fuss, Alina Bankal, Susan Hutt, Janice Back, ChatGPT, and Mary Ellen Jelen

About the Authors

Kim Sekas is an email marketing specialist, graphic designer, lifelong learner, and enthusiastic explorer of interesting ideas. When she isn't building email journeys or experimenting with AI, she's tending her garden, competing in VR fitness, knitting, or wandering down another fascinating tangent. She loves helping people feel comfortable with new technology and believes learning should be useful, laughing should be frequent, and getting unstuck is a skill anyone can learn.

Bill Jelen is the host of MrExcel.com, the author of 74 books about AI or Microsoft Excel, and a Microsoft MVP in Excel and Microsoft 365 Copilot. For more than two decades, he has helped people escape spreadsheet frustration, discover faster ways to work, and occasionally wonder why Excel made something so complicated in the first place. He has made more than 80 guest appearances on TV's *The Lab with Leo / Call for Help with Leo Laporte* and was voted guest of the year on the *Computer America* radio show. He enjoys experimenting with new technology, explaining difficult ideas in plain English, and reminding people that he is probably just as afraid of AI as they are.

Foreword

Both authors are members of the AM Crew, a dozen friends who meet virtually every morning at 5 AM to work out in VR. We put on our headsets, launch a fitness game called Supernatural, and spend 90 minutes swinging at virtual targets while sweating, laughing, and talking about work, family, travel, grandkids, sore muscles, and whatever else helps make the workout go faster.

Kim is a graphic designer, and was the first of us to dive into AI. Bill is an Excel guy who writes books about spreadsheets. At first, Bill remembers hearing Kim mention that she was taking an online class about writing better AI prompts. Then she started talking about a free Wednesday AI Meetup hosted by Emily Laird at the University of Wisconsin–Stout Polytechnic. Week after week, Kim encouraged Bill to attend.

What he finally found irresistible was: "This week, Justin Sullivan is talking about AI in Excel." That did it.

Imagine a dozen people who talk every morning. Our lives are not dominated by AI. We are not sitting around debating machine learning models or the future of humanity before sunrise. Mostly, we are trying to survive another workout.

But several times a week, someone would share a small AI story.

- "I asked ChatGPT to help write a tricky email."
- "I had it analyze my 401K and suggest investment strategy."
- "I found a hilarious prompt. You have to try this."

Someone would post a prompt in the AM Crew chat. A few others would try it. Then the answers would start rolling in. Sometimes they were useful. Sometimes they were ridiculous. Sometimes they were both.

That is how AI started to feel normal to us. Not because of a keynote speech. Not because of a corporate strategy memo but because a friend said, "Hey, try this," and suddenly everyone was laughing, learning, or getting unstuck.

Bill explains: My journey with AI went like this: January 1, 2023 at 1:28 PM, I asked my first ChatGPT question. I wanted to see if ChatGPT could write a somewhat advanced formula that I teach in my seminars. It did.

It took 11 days until I came back. I asked a legitimate Power Query question that I did not know the answer to, and then two more tough Excel questions that I did know the answer to. ChatGPT was successful on only one of three tasks that day.

A few weeks later, for some reason, I wondered if ChatGPT could write a limerick about Excel pivot tables. It worked!

During the rest of February 2023, I decided to only ask ChatGPT questions about Excel that I already knew the answer to, to see how often it was incorrect. I was probably trying to assess if ChatGPT was a threat to my livelihood. At that moment, it was not. But three years later, it would completely replace me.

By April 2023, I had discovered that Chat was great at writing. In August 2023, I learned that Chat was great at writing Python. Rather than having to learn Python, I would write a prompt in English and ChatGPT would write the Python code for me.

September 24, 2023 was my breakthrough moment. I asked ChatGPT to write a better title for a YouTube video and was very impressed with its suggestion. Soon, I was relying on Chat to write better YouTube titles, descriptions, and to correctly format the YouTube video transcripts. Fully 1/7th of my ChatGPT conversations to date have been to help me with my YouTube channel.

Even after finding a useful purpose for ChatGPT, I used it on only just seven days over the next two months, averaging 1.3 conversations on those days. In early 2024, I used it four days a month; by late 2024, that had risen to 9.5 days a month. In early 2025, I averaged 12.8 days a month and 1.5 conversations per active day. Two and a half years after my first experiment, I was using ChatGPT 23 days a month and having 77 conversations. So far in 2026, I use it 26 days a month and average 3.03 conversations per active day. My point? It took almost two and a half years for an occasional experiment to become a daily habit.

#1 What AI Can Do For You

Have you ever faced a problem like one of these:

- You get a strange letter from the insurance company and want someone to explain it.
- You have a gadget that mysteriously stops working and wonder what is the most common cause of the problem and what solutions other owners of the same gadget have used.
- You need to write a delicate email or letter. You want to sound kind, but firm.
- You have a houseplant that suddenly looks sick and wonder if it needs more light, more water, some pruning, or less pests.
- You wonder if your retirement money is invested wisely.
- You need to use a certain ingredient today and are wondering what dinner you can make from chicken, sun-dried tomatoes, and garlic but definitely not bell peppers since you are allergic to bell peppers.

These are all things that ChatGPT or Copilot or Claude or Grok or Gemini can help with.

You are not late to the party. Millions of smart people have never tried ChatGPT. You are not behind. You are right on time.

> In the summer of 2025, Bill wrote a somewhat technical book about creating custom instructions in ChatGPT. When his realtor Tony stopped by, Bill mentioned the book to Tony and handed him a copy to read. A few weeks later, Bill learned that Tony had never used ChatGPT before but is now using it to analyze real estate comps and his reverse mortgage. You will be amazed that you can find many useful things in your life that ChatGPT can help with and how quickly you will learn to write great prompts that get useful answers.

Getting Started with ChatGPT

Open your favorite browser, such as Chrome, Safari, or Edge. In the address bar, type ChatGPT.com and press Enter.

If this is your first time using ChatGPT, it might start with a screen like this, asking "Where should we begin?" Below that, is a box with a Plus sign and the suggestion to "Ask Anything".

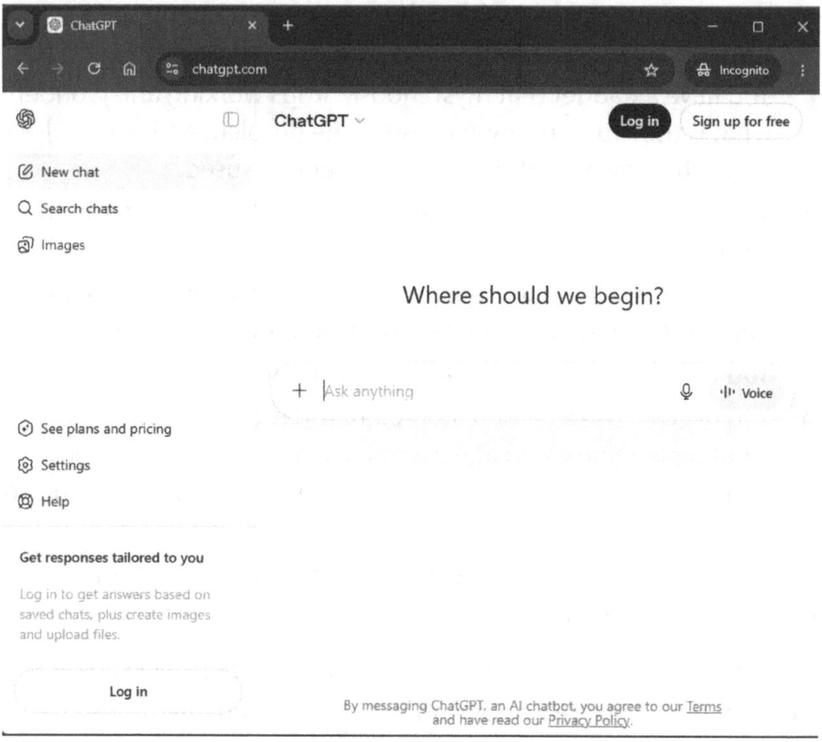

Start with something simple. Click in the Ask Anything box. Type the following and press Enter.

I am brand new to ChatGPT. Explain what I can do here in plain English, and give me five useful things I could try today.

Note: In this book, black boxes with white font represent parts of an AI conversation that the human typed. Grey boxes with black font are the responses from the AI Chatbot.

That command that you typed is called a "Prompt". Early in this book, we will teach you tips for writing great prompts that get great results.

I really want **you** to try ChatGPT, so I am not going to paste the entire response here. But I will summarize it. First, ChatGPT started with:

Think of ChatGPT as a conversational assistant that can help you learn, create, plan, analyze, and solve problems by chatting in natural language.

It gave me a list of 28 things it is good at. Then, it suggested five specific ideas:

- *I want to learn photography. Create a beginner plan for the next 30 days.*
- Paste an email and say *Make this clearer and more professional.*
- *Help me plan a weekend trip with a budget of $500*
- *I'm choosing between leasing and buying a car. What factors should I consider?*
- *Create a weekly meal plan with easy dinners*

Give More Details in Your Prompts

One of the suggestions above is *Help me plan a weekend trip for $500.* ChatGPT will certainly give you an answer for this question. But it does not know anything about you or where you live.

But, if you change the prompt to:

My spouse and I are in our fifties and live in Central Florida. We are looking for a weekend getaway to some Old Florida attractions that are a little funky and weird. Find a destination with some great local seafood restaurants and maybe some greenhouses where my wife can look for unusual plants.

This prompt gives ChatGPT enough information to come up with a useful recommendation. For me, it suggested:

Cedar Key feels like Florida before condos, theme parks, and chain restaurants. It's a tiny fishing and artist town at the end of a long road, with weathered docks, old cottages, funky galleries, clam boats, and spectacular Gulf sunsets.

ChatGPT then goes on for two pages. It lists four seafood restaurants. with a short description of each. It suggests funky things to do. It apologizes that there aren't many nurseries on Cedar Key, but suggests some that we can find on the drive home on Sunday.

Finally, it does a classic ChatGPT move, it suggests a way that you can stay engaged with ChatGPT.

> If you'd like, I can also suggest two other excellent Old Florida alternatives—one centered on Apalachicola (historic oyster town) and one around Everglades City (swampy, weird, and wonderfully offbeat)—and compare all three for driving time from Central Florida.

These suggestions at the end of ChatGPT's response are endearing. It is as if ChatGPT is saying "In case my suggestion completely missed the mark, I have other ideas." I like that. Sometimes, I will want to follow ChatGPT's suggested next step and I will answer with *yes*. But other times, I want to know more. It is fine to then ask a follow-up and ask *Can you suggest Cedar Key lodging?*

You Can Keep Talking

As shown in the previous example, the first answer that ChatGPT gives you is not the end. It is the beginning of the conversation. After reading ChatGPT's answer to any query, you can ask things like these:

- Make that simpler.
- Ask me three questions before giving advice.
- Give me three other options.
- That sounds too formal. Make it warmer.
- I don't understand that last paragraph. Explain it differently.

ChatGPT Can Get Things Wrong!

ChatGPT can help you comprehend, brainstorm, draft, and prepare. But, for medical, legal, tax, financial, or safety decisions, use it to get smarter questions — not as a final authority. When the AI chatbot confidently gives you the wrong answer, it is called a hallucination. Read more in "#33 Hallucinations: The ISPRIME Incident" on page 128.

Suggested: Create a Free Account

The bottom left of the ChatGPT window advises that if you create a free ChatGPT account, you can get responses that are tailored to you. In Chapter 2, we will walk you through creating this account. Both of us agree that this is a great first step.

Here is why:

- ChatGPT will ask your name. It can address you as "Kikas" or "MrExcel". Or even better, it could call you by your real first name!
- It will keep a history of past chats in the left margin of the window. These are really useful to revisit later. Just this morning, I needed to refer back to a months-old chat about my Magnavox record changer. When I searched for Magnavox and opened that old chat, I could continue asking new questions. If you type a prompt in an old chat, ChatGPT can usually use the earlier conversation as context, which makes it easier to pick up where you left off, even if it was months ago.

Next Steps

You have now done the most important thing: you asked ChatGPT a question and saw that it could give you a useful answer. You also saw that better details lead to better results.

In the next chapter, we will take one small but important step: creating a free ChatGPT account. That will let you save your conversations, return to useful answers later, and begin turning ChatGPT from a one-time novelty into a practical everyday helper.

#2 Set Up Your Free ChatGPT Account

The goal of this chapter is to get you signed in, comfortable, and ready to use the rest of the book.

Why Signing In Is Worth It

A year from now, you will be amazed at how well you and your Chatbot seem to know each other. But this only works if you sign in. It is free to create an account. Some benefits:

- Your past chats are available as Saved Conversations. It is easy to revisit a conversation from a month ago and pick up where you left off.
- You can personalize ChatGPT. You can control what it should call you and, in some cases, choose the attitude in which it should answer you.
- You will have fewer "Where did that old chat go?" moments.
- Eventually, if you decide to upgrade to paid Chat, you will need an account.

> Use the same common sense you would use with any online service. Do not type passwords, Social Security numbers, bank account numbers, private medical records, or anything you would not want stored in an internet account. The company who created ChatGPT is OpenAI. They publish a Privacy Policy and gives users data controls, including settings related to chat history, memory, and whether chats may be used to improve models. ChatGPT can be helpful without knowing everything about you. Share enough context to get a useful answer, but leave out details that are not needed.

Create a Free Account

To create your account, look in the top right of the ChatGPT window for something like "Sign Up For Free".

ChatGPT will offer to Continue with Google, Continue with Apple, Continue with Phone, or sign in using an email address. Choose your favorite method.

If you choose an email address, ChatGPT will send a verification code to that email box. Copy the code and paste it into ChatGPT.

Your final step is to enter a name and an age.

ChatGPT asks for your age because it is not intended for very young children, and younger users may need parental permission or extra safety protections. This is not unusual for online services. If you are an adult, enter your real age and continue. If you are helping a teenager sign up, check the current rules and make sure a parent or guardian is involved.

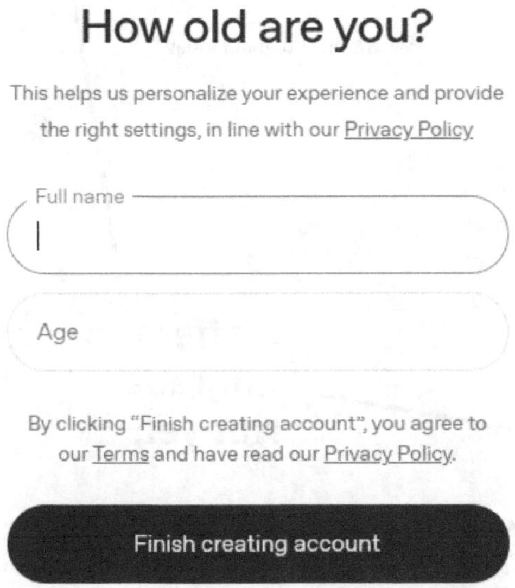

ChatGPT may ask, *What brings you to ChatGPT today?* with choices such as School, Work, Personal Tasks, Fun and Entertainment, or Other. This is not a test. Pick the closest answer, or skip it if you would rather not answer. For most readers of this book, Personal Tasks is a good choice because we will use ChatGPT for everyday questions, planning, writing, learning, making decisions, and getting unstuck.

Your choice here does not lock you into anything. If you choose Personal Tasks today, you can still ask work questions, school questions, silly questions, and everything else later.

Your First Signed-In Chat

Browse to ChatGPT.com. Your screen might look something like this one. In the lower left corner, you will see that you are signed in and using a Free account.

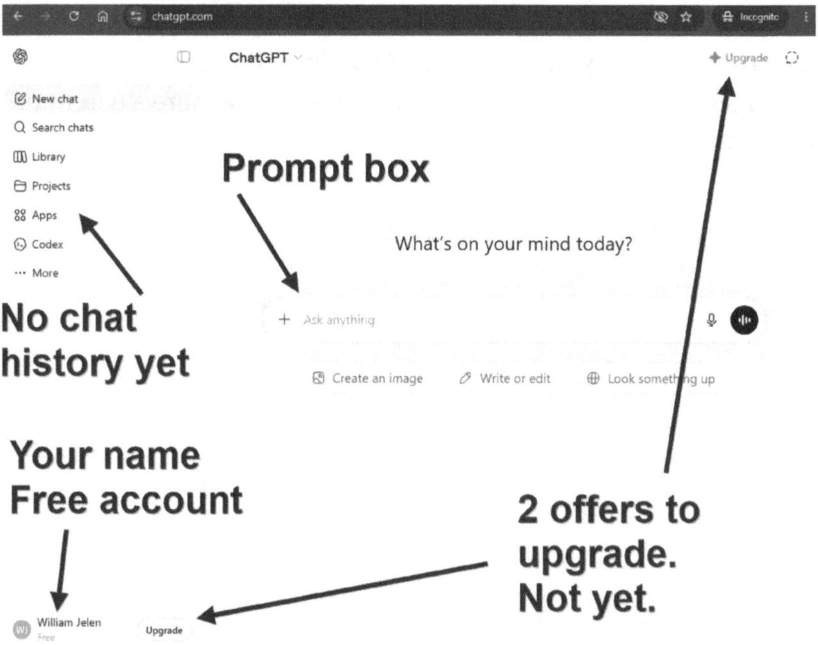

The Prompt Box still says Ask Anything, but the line above it now says What's On Your Mind Today?

Note that your prompt from Chapter 1 does NOT show up in the left sidebar. That chat happened when you were not signed in. This first chat from Chapter 2 will be the first that appears in Chat History.

There are also two links encouraging you to upgrade. You may be ready by the end of this book. But for right now, the free version is powerful enough.

You can ask ChatGPT to ask questions before answering. Click in the Prompt box and type this prompt.

I am new to ChatGPT and I am not sure what to ask. Interview me for a few minutes, one question at a time, then suggest practical, fun, and surprising ways you could help me.

This was a fascinating exercise for me. I answered the questions. ChatGPT gave me a list of ten ideas. Some are related to book creation. But here is one that I found fascinating:

Ask Bill from another universe. You can ask *How would 2005 Bill answer this? How would 2026 Bill answer this?* This is surprisingly useful for determining how solutions evolve.

The Left Sidebar / Chat History

When signed in, all chats that you have created will appear in the left sidebar. If you need to revisit a chat later, you can either scroll through past chats and click the chat, or use the Search Chats at the top of the left sidebar.

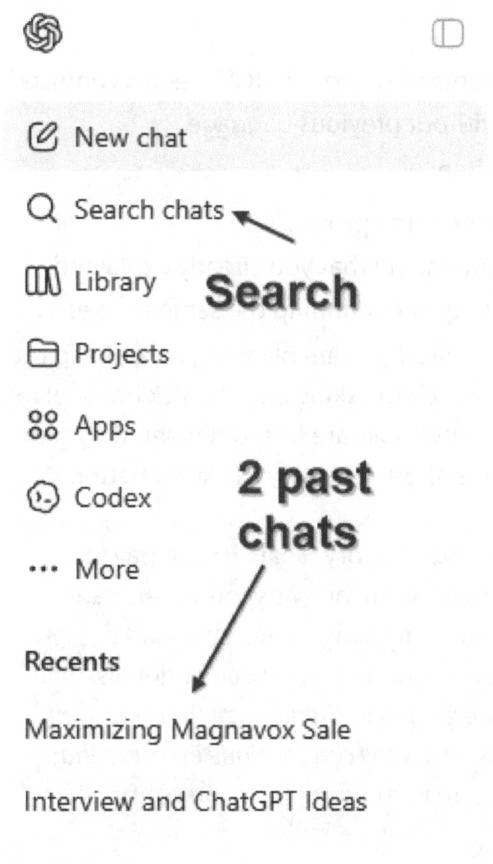

Rename Chats

This is a small but useful habit: During a chat, ChatGPT gives the chat a name. In the image above, the names are "Maximizing Magnavox Sale" and "Interview and ChatGPT Ideas".

Months from now, I might not remember the "Interview and ChatGPT Ideas" chat as the one where ChatGPT gave me specific ideas for generating revenue from old Excel books. If I renamed it as "Generating revenue from old Excel books" I will be able to more easily find it later.

When you hover over a chat in the Recents panel, a set of three dots appears in the top right. Click the dots and choose Rename.

Start a New Chat or Continue an Old One?

When should you start a new chat? Start a new chat when:

- You are switching topics
- The conversation has become huge or ChatGPT seems confused
- You want to start over without previous baggage

Keep using the same chat when:

- You are still working on the same project
- You want ChatGPT to remember what you already explained
- You are revising, improving, or continuing the same answer.

Think of each chat as a notebook. If you are planning a trip, keep the trip in one notebook. If you switch to asking about a sick houseplant, start a new notebook. Long notebooks are fine, but when they get messy, a fresh notebook plus a short summary can work better.

> **Tip**: Each chat has a working memory. ChatGPT can pay attention to the recent conversation, but very long chats can eventually become harder for it to follow. If a chat starts wandering, getting confused, or forgetting earlier details, ask, *This conversation is getting long. Summarize the important facts, decisions, and instructions so I can continue in a new chat.* Then start a new chat, paste in the summary, and continue

from there. This is more reliable than simply asking the new chat to refer to the old one.

A tiny intro to personalization

Once you have an account, ChatGPT can begin to feel a little less like a blank search box and a little more like a helpful assistant.

For example, you can tell it what name to call you. You can ask for shorter answers, friendlier answers, or plain-English explanations. Over time, ChatGPT may also remember useful preferences, such as topics you care about or how you like answers presented.

You do not have to personalize anything right now. The important thing is simply this: signing in gives ChatGPT a better chance of helping you in a way that fits you.

Later in this book, we will show you how to review and control these personalization settings. For now, just know that you are not locked into anything. You can change these settings later, and you should still avoid sharing private details that ChatGPT does not need.

How to Make Free ChatGPT Better

Right now when you start using the free version of ChatGPT, its memory only lasts as long as the current chat. So you can type a prompt and it gives you an answer. And then you can type more prompts and it will have a conversation. But once that chat is over, the next chat won't remember anything that happened in that first chat.

There is a setting to allow ChatGPT to have persistent memories about you. If you open ChatGPT on the web, in the lower left hand corner, click on your picture. Then go to Profile. On the left side of Profile, go to Personalization. And there's a section there called Memory.

There are two settings - One is to allow ChatGPT to reference saved memories. That should be available to everybody. And then a setting for Chat History - this might not be available to the free accounts. Turn on both of those if you can.

If they're already on, there's a Manage Memories button. Click Manage. And you can see what is remembered about you. You can always come back here and have it delete any particular memory or it can delete all memories about you.

If either of those settings are on, you can prompt ChatGPT with, *Surprise me. Tell me 10 persistent memories you know about me.*

In fact, you can even ask it to remember a specific fact. Sometimes I ask ChatGPT for recipes. And I need to make sure that those recipes never have bell peppers, because MrsExcel is allergic to bell peppers. So I could type a prompt: *Remember that my wife Mary Ellen is allergic to bell peppers.* And it will remember that and future recipes will be free of bell peppers.

If you are freaked out that ChatGPT has memories about you, we'll discuss in more depth in "#32 Memory" on page 125. For now, realize that if you're ever uncomfortable, you can go and have it remove specific memories or remove all the memories. It's all under your control.

Next Steps

You now have a ChatGPT account, you know where your chats are saved, and you know how to start fresh when a conversation gets too messy. That is enough setup for now.

It is time to use ChatGPT for something more interesting.

#3 Learning With ChatGPT

ChatGPT can be far more than a place to look up answers. It can become a patient tutor, a study partner, and a coach that adjusts to the way you learn best. In this section, you will see just how many subjects ChatGPT can help with, then learn how to ask for explanations at your level, turn documents and ideas into lessons, quiz yourself, and work through problems one step at a time. The goal is not simply to get an answer. It is to understand something better than you did before.

#4 ChatGPT is a Master of Many Topics

As I started using ChatGPT frequently to help me create YouTube videos about Excel, I naturally accepted that ChatGPT knows a lot about Excel and Excel VBA.

I am not sure why I was always surprised to find that ChatGPT is just as well trained on a million other topics. I might be talking to someone else and they say that they learned X in a conversation with ChatGPT. The following examples will give you a sense of the breadth of ChatGPT's knowledge.

Decoding Old-Time Handwriting

Kim had mentioned that she was looking through some old ship logs on Ancestry.com. She mentioned how the cursive handwriting was different 200 years ago. Kim snapped a photo of the handwriting. She uploaded the photo to ChatGPT and asked it to translate the old time handwriting to text. It did amazingly well.

My wife and her siblings were trying to make their mom's chicken rollups. The cursive handwriting, while not ancient, was hard to read. I snapped a photo and uploaded it to ChatGPT.

> This recipe is in old fashioned cursive. Can you extract the recipe?

ChatGPT extracted the text and let me know if there were any parts that it was unsure about. For the parts where it was unsure, it used reasoning to figure out what might go there.

> The first ingredient could possibly read "3 oz cheese softened", but it strongly appears to be cream cheese, softened, which is a common ingredient in chicken crescent-roll recipes.
>
> The instruction line likely says "Blend cheese & melted butter", though there isn't a butter amount listed in the ingredients.
>
> If you'd like, I can estimate the missing butter amount based on similar vintage chicken crescent-roll recipes.

Troubleshooting Gadgets

We have two video monitors to keep an eye on a vacant condo. Suddenly, one of the two monitors could no longer connect to wifi. I found the model number on the bottom of the unit. I described to ChatGPT the model number and how one unit would connect to wifi and the other would not.

ChatGPT suggested that I try a new power supply and gave an explanation about this model failing to connect to wifi without full power. I honestly thought it was a stupid suggestion and ignored it. We bought a new camera. Mary Ellen installed the camera with the old power supply and it would not connect to wifi either.

At this point, shaking my head, I said, this seems insane, but lets try the new power adapter with the old camera. It worked. After this, all troubleshooting goes through ChatGPT first and I listen instead of ignoring.

Check Engine Light

One of our cars is ten years old and I will sometimes get a check engine light. My mechanic friend Cy told me to buy a BlueDriver scanner to get the codes behind the check engine light.

I go to ChatGPT with the year, make, and model of the car and the codes reported by BlueDriver. It suggests what it likely means and gives me talking points to ask the mechanic when getting the car fixed.

Health Test Results

Later in this book, we will tell you that ChatGPT is not a replacement for a doctor or a lawyer. But I will tell you that ChatGPT helps me organize questions for my doctor. Our local hospital switched over to a system called MyChart. It is amazing how fast test results are posted to MyChart.

Typically, a doctor will order some tests and then schedule a follow up appointment to discuss the results. I copy the test results from MyChart and paste into a prompt in ChatGPT.

> I am seeing my doctor this week to discuss this medical test. What questions should I ask?

Without giving medical advice, ChatGPT is excellent at organizing which questions to ask.

Getting V.A. Benefits

Here in the US, the Veteran's Affairs has an amazing network of hospitals for veterans. If the former service member can show that a medical condition is due to something that happened in the service, the treatment is covered. I was having dinner with a veteran, who explained how he sent details of the medical condition and his service history to ChatGPT. The chatbot was able to explain the most likely path for the V.A. to approve the treatment. *[This aspect] of your service is frequently a cause of [this aspect] of your condition. That is your strongest argument on the request.* He put ChatGPT's advice to use, and he was approved.

Gardening Advice

Kim has uploaded photos of an apple tree in her yard. She had the exact variety from the original tag. ChatGPT was able to give her pruning advice, specific to her tree.

Custom Recipes

ChatGPT can help with recipe creation.

> We are making fish tacos with pineapple salsa. We are allergic to bell peppers. Include roasted corn. I don't want the salsa to be too spicy. Can you suggest a recipe for the salsa?

It is also great at changing existing recipes. *I am out of this ingredient. What can I substitute?* Or - *I need to add more grams of protein to this recipe.*

Next Steps

In the next chapter, we will start with one of the most useful things ChatGPT can do: help you learn. Not by dumping a textbook on your screen, but by explaining things in plain English, answering follow-up questions, giving examples, and patiently trying again when the first explanation does not land.

You are about to meet ChatGPT the tutor.

#5 ChatGPT as a Patient Tutor

Have you ever avoided asking a question because you were afraid it was too basic?

Maybe someone was explaining a new phone, a financial statement, or a feature in Excel. Everyone else seemed to understand, so you nodded along. Meanwhile, a small voice in your head was saying, "I have no idea what any of these people are talking about."

That is one of the best things about learning with ChatGPT. It does not become impatient. It does not sigh. It does not look at the clock. It does not say, "We covered this yesterday."

You can ask the same question five different ways. You can admit that the first explanation made no sense. You can ask it to slow down, use simpler words, provide an example, or compare the topic to something you already understand.

You never have to pretend that you understand.

ChatGPT can help you learn almost anything: how interest rates work, why the moon changes shape, what a word means, how a car engine works, why your houseplant is losing leaves, or how to use a feature in a computer program.

It can also adjust the lesson to fit you. This is different from searching the internet. A search engine gives you a list of pages that someone else wrote for a general audience. ChatGPT can give you an explanation created for your question, your experience level, and the way that you prefer to learn.

The important trick is to treat ChatGPT as a tutor, not as an encyclopedia. Do not ask one question, read one answer, and leave. Have a conversation.

Ask It to Explain It Your Way

Imagine that someone tells you that your mortgage uses amortization. You could ask ChatGPT: *Explain mortgage amortization.*

That will probably produce a useful answer. But it might sound like something copied from a finance textbook. You might see phrases such as principal allocation, declining interest expense, and repayment schedule. There is nothing wrong with those terms. But if you are brand new to the topic, the explanation might not help.

Try this instead: *Explain mortgage amortization in plain English. Assume I know nothing about mortgages. Use an example with simple numbers.*

Now ChatGPT knows three important things:

- You want plain English.
- You are a beginner.
- You want an example.

It might explain that each mortgage payment contains two parts. One part pays interest to the lender. The other part reduces the amount that you owe. Early in the loan, more of the payment goes toward interest. Later, more of it goes toward paying down the loan.

That is already better. But suppose it still does not click. Keep going: *Why does more money go toward interest at the beginning?*

ChatGPT can explain that the interest is calculated using the amount that you still owe. At the beginning, you owe almost the entire loan balance, so the interest charge is larger. As the balance falls, the interest charge falls.

You could then say: *Show me the first three monthly payments on a $100,000 loan. Round the numbers so they are easy to follow.* Now you are not simply reading a definition. You are building your understanding one question at a time.

You can ask ChatGPT to explain a topic using something that you already know. For example:

- *Explain compound interest using a snowball rolling downhill.*
- *Explain computer memory by comparing it to a desk and a filing cabinet.*
- *Explain the stock market using a farmers market.*
- *Explain electricity as if water were flowing through pipes.*

You can also tell ChatGPT what kind of learner you are:

- *I learn best from examples.*
- *Give me a visual analogy.*
- *Explain this as a short story.*
- *Walk me through it step by step.*
- *Give me the big picture first, then explain the details.*
- *Skip the history and show me how this works in real life.*
- *Do not use technical words unless you define them.*

This is one of the biggest advantages of using ChatGPT as a tutor. A book has one explanation printed on the page. A video has one explanation recorded in advance. ChatGPT can keep changing the explanation until you find one that works for you.

Suppose you are trying to understand inflation. You could begin with: *Explain inflation in plain English.*

Then continue: *Why do prices rise during inflation? Who benefits from inflation? Who is hurt by inflation? Why can wages rise without making people feel richer? Give me an example using the price of a hamburger. Quiz me with three questions to see if I understand.*

You have turned one question into a miniature lesson.

You can also control how much information you receive. ChatGPT has a tendency to be helpful. Sometimes it becomes a little too helpful. You ask what time the movie starts, and it wants to explain the history of motion pictures. When that happens, say: *Give me the 30-second explanation.* Or: *Explain this in one paragraph.* Or: *Start with the simplest possible explanation. I will ask for more detail if I need it.*

This is useful when you are learning a difficult subject. You do not need the entire textbook dropped on your head at once. Start with one idea. Understand it. Then move to the next idea.

Keep Asking Until It Clicks

There is a moment in school that many people remember. The teacher explains something. You do not understand. You raise your hand

and ask a question. The teacher repeats the exact same explanation, only louder. That is not particularly useful.

With ChatGPT, you can specifically ask for a different explanation: *That did not make sense to me. Explain it in a completely different way.*

This is a powerful prompt. You are not saying that the topic is impossible. You are saying that the first road did not reach the destination. Try another road.

You could also say: *I understand the first part, but you lost me when you started talking about interest rates. Explain only that part.*

What is the one idea I need to understand before the rest of this will make sense? Give me a simpler example. Show me a common mistake people make. Ask me a question to figure out which part I do not understand.

That last prompt is particularly interesting. Instead of asking ChatGPT to keep talking, ask it to diagnose the confusion. For example: *I am trying to understand the difference between saving and investing, but the explanations are not sticking. Ask me three questions, one at a time, to figure out what I am missing.*

ChatGPT might discover that you think all investing involves buying individual stocks. Once it understands the misconception, it can explain savings accounts, bonds, mutual funds, and other choices more clearly.

You can also ask ChatGPT to teach you by asking questions instead of giving answers. Try: *Teach me about the causes of the Civil War. Ask me one question at a time. Let me answer before you continue. Correct me when I am wrong, but do not make me feel stupid.*

Or: *Help me learn basic Italian for an upcoming trip. Give me one useful phrase at a time, then ask me to use it in a sentence.*

Or: *Teach me how percentages work. Do not give me the answer immediately. Give me a hint and let me try.*

This changes ChatGPT from a lecturer into a coach.

There is a danger in learning from any helpful tool: it can be tempting to let the tool do all the work. If you ask ChatGPT to solve every problem, write every answer, and complete every assignment, you might finish the task without learning very much.

A better prompt is: *Do not solve this for me. Help me figure it out.* That one sentence changes the entire conversation.

You can ask for hints: *Give me one hint. Tell me whether I am on the right track. Point out the first mistake, but let me fix it. Ask me what I think the next step should be. Give me a similar practice problem.*

This is particularly useful for math, computer programming, grammar, and anything else where you improve by doing.

ChatGPT can also create a learning plan. Suppose you inherited a camera with a collection of mysterious buttons and dials. You could say: *I have a digital camera, but I have always used it in automatic mode. Create a seven-day beginner plan to teach me aperture, shutter speed, and ISO. Give me one short lesson and one practice assignment each day.*

Or: *I want to understand basic home electrical systems so I can speak intelligently with an electrician. I do not plan to do dangerous repairs myself. Create a beginner lesson covering the important terms and safety rules.*

Notice the safety language in that prompt. ChatGPT can teach you about electricity, health, legal topics, investing, and many other serious subjects. But it can also make mistakes. Use it to learn the vocabulary, understand the big ideas, and prepare smarter questions. Do not treat it as the final authority when a mistake could cost you money, damage your house, or send you to the emergency room.

When the subject matters, ask: *How confident are you in this explanation? What parts should I verify? Give me the names of reliable sources I should check. What questions should I ask a qualified professional?*

Being a patient tutor does not mean being a perfect tutor. Still, ChatGPT gives you something that was difficult to find before: a private place to be confused. You can ask the question that everyone else seems to know. You can ask for the children's version first and the adult version later. You can say, *I still do not get it.* You can make it start over. And you can keep going until the little light finally comes on. That is learning.

#6 Learn at Your Own Level

One of the hardest things about learning is finding the right starting point. A lesson can be too basic. You already understand the first half, so you become bored before reaching the useful part.

Or the lesson can begin three floors above your head. The teacher starts using terms that everyone else apparently learned years ago, and you are lost before the second paragraph.

ChatGPT can adjust. You can tell it what you already know, what you do not know, and how much detail you want. Instead of accepting a one-size-fits-all explanation, you can ask for an explanation that starts at your level.

This sounds simple, but it makes a huge difference.

Suppose you want to learn about investing. There is no single correct beginner level. One person might not know the difference between a stock and a bond. Another person might already own mutual funds but not understand expense ratios. Someone else might understand all of that but want to learn about tax-loss harvesting.

All three people could ask: *Teach me about investing.* But they need three completely different answers. The better approach is to tell ChatGPT where you are starting.

Tell ChatGPT What You Already Know

The easiest way to get a better lesson is to add one sentence explaining your experience. For example: *Explain investing to me like I am a complete beginner. I do not know the difference between a stock, a bond, and a mutual fund.*

Or: *I understand stocks, bonds, and mutual funds. Skip those basics and explain index funds and expense ratios.*

Or: *I have been investing for twenty years. Explain tax-loss harvesting and include the important limitations.*

Each prompt asks about investing, but each one establishes a different starting line.

You can use this technique for almost any subject:

- *I know how to take photos in automatic mode, but I do not understand aperture, shutter speed, or ISO.*
- *I can cook basic meals, but I want to learn how to build sauces without following a recipe.*
- *I understand simple Excel formulas such as SUM and AVERAGE, but I have never used XLOOKUP.*
- *I know the basic rules of baseball, but I do not understand advanced statistics.*
- *I studied Spanish years ago. I remember common words, but I am rusty with grammar and conversation.*

The phrase "I already know…" is enormously useful. So is the phrase "I do not know…" You might say:

- *I already understand how credit cards work, but I do not understand how credit scores are calculated.*
- *I know what inflation is, but I do not understand why raising interest rates might slow it down.*
- *I understand that artificial intelligence learns from data, but I do not understand what a language model actually does.*

These prompts prevent ChatGPT from wasting time explaining things that you already understand. They also help it identify the missing bridge between what you know and what you are trying to learn. You can be very direct:

- *Do not explain the basics.*
- *Skip the history.*
- *Assume I know the terminology.*
- *Start from zero.*
- *Use no jargon.*
- *Define every technical word.*
- *Give me the executive summary first.*
- *Teach this at a college level.*
- *Teach this at a middle-school level.*

Those are not insults to your intelligence. They are instructions about the lesson.

Sometimes people resist asking for a beginner explanation because they think "beginner" means "stupid." It does not.

I am an Excel expert. I can talk about formulas, pivot tables, and macros for hours. But if you ask me to repair an air-conditioning system, I am a beginner. If you ask an air-conditioning technician to build a complicated Excel dashboard, that person might be the beginner. Everyone is a beginner somewhere.

The useful question is not, "Am I smart enough to understand this?" The useful question is, "Where should this explanation begin?" You can also ask ChatGPT to check your level before teaching you.

Try: *I want to learn about photography. Ask me five questions, one at a time, to figure out what I already know. Then suggest where I should begin.*

Or: *I want to learn basic accounting. Give me a short diagnostic quiz, then create a lesson based on my answers.*

This is useful when you are not sure how much you know. You might discover that you understand more than you thought. Or you might discover one missing idea that is making everything else confusing.

For example, someone learning Excel formulas might understand how to type a formula but not understand relative and absolute references. That one missing concept can make copying formulas seem mysterious. ChatGPT can spot the gap and build the lesson around it.

Ask for an Explanation That Fits You

Your experience level is only one way to tailor a lesson. You can also tell ChatGPT how you think. *I like analogies. If someone can compare a new subject to Excel, there is a good chance I will understand it.*

For example: *Teach me how a database works using an Excel workbook as the analogy.*

ChatGPT might explain that a database table is similar to an Excel table. Each row represents a record. Each column stores one type of information. A unique identification number works like a customer ID that prevents two people named John Smith from becoming mixed together. That gives me a familiar structure for understanding something new.

You can ask ChatGPT to use any subject that you already know:

- *Explain computer memory using a kitchen.*
- *Explain the federal budget using a household budget.*
- *Explain a computer network using roads and traffic.*
- *Explain DNA using a recipe book.*
- *Explain supply and demand using tickets to a sold-out concert.*
- *Explain this using baseball.*
- *Explain this using gardening.*
- *Explain this using a small business.*

The analogy does not have to be perfect. Its job is to give your brain something familiar to hold while you examine the new idea.

You can also tailor the format. Some people want the big picture before the details: *Give me a one-paragraph overview first. Then explain each part.*

Other people want to begin with a real-world example: *Start with an example, then explain the rule behind it.*

Some people prefer a sequence: *Teach me this in five steps.*

Others learn through comparison: *Create a table comparing these three options.*

You might want pictures: *Describe a simple diagram that would help me understand this.*

Or repetition: *After each section, summarize the main idea in one sentence.*

Or practice: *Give me a short exercise after each concept.*

Or conversation: *Teach me by asking questions instead of lecturing.*

This is why ChatGPT can be so useful as a learning tool. It does not merely change the facts in the explanation. It can change the shape of the explanation.

Suppose you are trying to understand how a reverse mortgage works. You could ask: *Explain a reverse mortgage.*

But you might get a broad answer covering eligibility, equity, interest, fees, repayment, heirs, taxes, insurance, and government rules all at once.

A more tailored prompt would be: *I understand a regular mortgage, but reverse mortgages confuse me. Explain the differences using a simple example of a homeowner who has paid off most of the house. Start with the big picture and avoid legal terminology.*

Now ChatGPT knows what comparison to use, what you already understand, what example would help, and what language to avoid.

After reading the answer, you can adjust again: *I understand how the homeowner receives money. I do not understand when the loan has to be repaid.*

Or: *Explain what happens to the house after the homeowner dies.*

Or: *Now give me the five most important questions to ask a reverse-mortgage professional.*

The lesson grows with you. As soon as you understand one layer, you can ask for the next one.

You can say: *That makes sense. Go one level deeper. Now explain the technical version. What important detail did you leave out of the beginner explanation? Show me an exception to the general rule. Give me a more realistic example.*

This is a good way to avoid two common problems.

- The first problem is receiving too much information too soon.
- The second problem is staying with an oversimplified explanation after you are ready for more.

ChatGPT can begin simply without leaving you stuck at the simple level forever. You can climb one step at a time.

There is another benefit to telling ChatGPT what you already know. It makes it easier to notice when ChatGPT has misunderstood you.

Suppose you say: *I have used Excel for years, but I have never written a macro. Teach me the basics of VBA.*

If ChatGPT begins by explaining how to enter numbers in cells, you can immediately correct it: *I am not an Excel beginner. Skip worksheet basics. I am only new to VBA.* You are allowed to steer the lesson. You can stop it. You can redirect it. You can say that the answer is too easy, too hard, too long, too vague, or too technical.

A classroom teacher may be trying to teach thirty people at once. A book has to choose one path for every reader. A video keeps playing whether you understand it or not. ChatGPT can change course for one student. **You.**

A useful starter prompt is:

> I want to learn about [topic]. Here is what I already know: [brief explanation]. Here is what confuses me: [brief explanation]. Teach me at the right level, using [examples, analogies, steps, questions, or another preferred method].

For example:

> I want to learn about artificial intelligence. I understand that computers are trained using data, but I do not understand how ChatGPT predicts words. Teach me at a beginner level using an Excel analogy, and stop after each major idea so I can ask questions.

That prompt gives ChatGPT a map. It shows where you are, where you want to go, and which road might work best. Learning becomes easier when the lesson meets you at the right place. Not five miles behind you. Not five miles ahead of you. Right where you are.

#7 Turn Anything Into a Lesson

Most of us are surrounded by things we do not completely understand.

A letter from the insurance company arrives with three paragraphs of legal-sounding language. A news article assumes that you already understand inflation, tariffs, or artificial intelligence. A repair manual uses six unfamiliar terms in the first sentence. A financial statement is full of numbers that look important, but you are not sure which ones matter.

You could search the internet for each unfamiliar word. You could read three other articles. You could call someone and hope they have time to explain it.

Or you could hand the whole thing to ChatGPT and say: *Teach me what this means.* That is one of the most useful ways to learn with ChatGPT. You do not have to begin with a textbook or a carefully designed course. You can begin with whatever is sitting in front of you.

- Paste an article.
- Upload a document.
- Take a photo of a page.
- Describe the confusing part.

Then ask ChatGPT to turn it into a lesson.

Start With the Material in Front of You

Suppose you receive a letter from your homeowner's insurance company. You read it twice. You recognize all the individual words, but together they seem to form some sort of secret insurance language.

You could paste the letter into ChatGPT and say: *Explain this letter in plain English. Tell me what changed, what action I need to take, and what deadline matters.*

That is already better than simply asking: What does this mean?

The more specific prompt tells ChatGPT how to organize the answer.

It might respond with: The company is changing your deductible. The new deductible begins at your next renewal. You do not need to respond unless you want to shop for a different policy. The most important date is October 1.

Suddenly, a page of insurance language becomes four understandable points. You can then continue: *What is a deductible? Give me an example using a $12,000 roof repair. What question should I ask my insurance agent? Is there anything in this letter that I might be overlooking?* Now the document has become a lesson about insurance.

You can do the same thing with an article. Suppose a news story says that the Federal Reserve may keep interest rates high because inflation remains stubborn. You could paste the article and ask:

> Summarize this article in five bullet points. Define any financial terms that an average reader might not know. Then explain why this matters to someone with a mortgage, savings account, and credit card debt.

That prompt does several jobs.

- It asks for a summary.
- It asks for definitions.
- It asks for practical meaning.

You are not merely shortening the article. You are connecting it to your life.

You can also ask ChatGPT to separate facts from interpretation: *Which parts of this article are facts? Which parts are the writer's analysis or opinion? What assumptions does the writer make? What important questions does the article not answer?* This is particularly useful when reading complicated news, opinion pieces, political commentary, or financial predictions.

ChatGPT can help you understand the structure of an argument instead of simply accepting it. You can upload a document and say: *Teach this document to me as if I will need to explain it to someone else tomorrow.*

That request changes the goal. ChatGPT is no longer just summarizing. It is helping you prepare to understand and repeat the main ideas.

You could ask: *What are the three most important ideas? What terms do I need to understand? Create a simple example for each idea. What questions might someone ask me after I explain this? Give me a short quiz at the end.*

This works for reports, contracts, meeting notes, instruction manuals, school material, research papers, and many other documents.

Of course, use common sense with private information. Remove account numbers, Social Security numbers, passwords, medical identification numbers, and other details that ChatGPT does not need.

You can usually get a useful explanation without including every private detail. For example: *This is a medical bill. Explain the categories and help me identify questions to ask the billing office.* You do not need to include your full patient number.

Or: *This is a retirement-plan document. Explain the fees and investment choices.* You do not need to include every account number or current balance.

Share enough to understand the material, but not more than necessary.

You can also use a photo. Suppose you find an old handwritten recipe. Take a clear picture and upload it by using the + sign in the prompt box. Then ask: *Extract the recipe from this image. Mark any words you are unsure about. Rewrite the instructions in a clear modern format.*

ChatGPT may be able to read the handwriting, organize the ingredients, and point out a missing oven temperature. You can then say:

- *Based on similar recipes, what oven temperature was probably intended?*
- *Why does this recipe use cream cheese?*
- *Can I make it ahead of time?*

Now the old recipe has become a lesson in cooking.

The same approach works with charts, labels, diagrams, equipment panels, and screenshots. You might upload a photo of the controls on an unfamiliar appliance and ask: *Explain what each button probably does. Start with the controls I am most likely to use.*

Or upload a chart from a report: *Explain this chart in plain English. What is the main trend? What would be an easy mistake to make when reading it?* That last question is important.

Charts can be technically accurate and still be misleading. The scale might begin at 95 instead of zero. Two lines might look close even though they use different measurements. A percentage increase might sound dramatic even though the original number was tiny.

ChatGPT can help you slow down and ask better questions.

Ask ChatGPT to Teach It Back to You

A summary is useful, but a lesson goes further. A summary tells you what the material says. A lesson helps you understand why it matters, how the ideas connect, and whether you can explain them yourself.

After pasting or uploading something, try: *Do not just summarize this. Teach it to me.* Then add instructions about how you want to learn:

- *Start with the big picture.*
- *Define unfamiliar terms as they appear.*
- *Use simple examples.*
- *Explain one section at a time.*
- *Stop after each section and ask whether I am ready to continue.*
- *Give me an analogy.*
- *Point out the most important idea.*
- *Tell me what is safe to ignore on a first reading.*

That final prompt can be surprisingly useful.

Some documents contain ten pages of detail, but only three ideas matter to a beginner. ChatGPT can help you avoid drowning in information before you understand the main point.

Suppose you upload a document explaining how solar panels work. You could ask: *Teach me this document in three levels. Level 1: Give me the big idea in one paragraph. Level 2: Explain the five most important concepts. Level 3: Explain the technical details I should learn next.* This lets you choose how deep to go. You might discover that Level 1 is enough. Or you might become curious and continue.

ChatGPT can also create examples that are easier than the ones in the original material. Suppose a document explains compound interest using a complicated investment account with monthly contributions, changing rates, and taxes.

You could say: *The example in this document is too complicated. Create a simpler example using $1,000 and a fixed interest rate.*

Or: *Show me a real-world example of this idea.*

Or: *Give me an example where this concept goes wrong.*

Examples are often the bridge between reading words and actually understanding the idea.

You can also ask ChatGPT to identify what you need to know first.

Try: *What background knowledge does this document assume?* That question can reveal why something feels confusing. Maybe an article about artificial intelligence assumes that you understand algorithms, training data, and probability. Maybe a financial document assumes that you know the difference between revenue and profit. Maybe a gardening guide assumes that you know what well-drained soil means.

Once ChatGPT identifies the missing background, you can say: *Teach me those three ideas first, then return to the document.* This is much better than struggling through material that begins in the middle.

You can also ask ChatGPT to test whether you understood it. After the lesson, say: *Ask me five questions, one at a time, to see whether I understood the main ideas.*

Or: *Ask me to explain this in my own words, then tell me what I missed.*

Or: *Give me three true-or-false questions that target common misunderstandings.*

Or: *Create a short practice problem based on this material.*

This turns passive reading into active learning. There is a big difference between recognizing an explanation and being able to produce one yourself. You may read a paragraph and think, "Yes, that makes sense." Then someone asks you to explain it, and your mind goes blank. ChatGPT can help you practice that step.

Try: *Pretend you are my neighbor and ask me to explain this topic in plain English.* Then answer the question yourself.

ChatGPT can respond: *You explained the main idea correctly, but you left out why the interest rate matters.* That kind of feedback is useful because it shows you exactly where your understanding is incomplete.

You can even ask ChatGPT to create a study guide from almost anything. For example: *Turn this article into a one-page study guide with key terms, main ideas, examples, and five review questions.*

Or: *Turn these meeting notes into a lesson for someone who missed the meeting.*

Or: *Turn this instruction manual into a beginner checklist.*

Or: *Turn this chapter into flash cards.*

The original material does not have to be designed for teaching. ChatGPT can reorganize it into something easier to learn. This is especially valuable when the material was written by an expert. Experts often forget what beginners do not know. They use abbreviations without defining them. They skip steps that seem obvious. They explain the exception before the beginner understands the rule. ChatGPT can act as the translator between expert language and beginner understanding.

You can say: *This was written for experts. Rewrite the explanation for an intelligent beginner.* That phrase - **an intelligent beginner** - is useful.

You are not asking ChatGPT to make the idea childish. You are asking it to remove unnecessary jargon and fill in missing steps.

There is one caution. ChatGPT can misunderstand a document. It can miss a qualification, oversimplify a legal clause, or confidently explain something incorrectly. For important material, ask it to stay close to the source. For example, *base your answer only on the document I provided. If the document does not answer something, say so.*

You can also ask:

- *Quote the section that supports each major conclusion.*
- *What parts of your explanation are directly stated in the document?*
- *What parts are your interpretation?*
- *What should I verify with a professional?*

Those prompts are particularly important for legal, medical, tax, safety, and financial documents. Use ChatGPT to understand the material and prepare better questions. Do not let it make the final high-stakes decision for you.

Still, think about how powerful this is. A confusing article can become a lesson. A dense report can become a study guide. A handwritten recipe can become clear instructions. A chart can become a conversation. A technical document can become a beginner's explanation.

You no longer have to wait for someone else to create the perfect lesson. You can start with whatever you already have. Then ask ChatGPT to teach it back to you.

#8 Quiz Me Until I Know It

There is a big difference between reading something and knowing it. You can read a chapter, nod along, and think, "Yes, that all makes sense." Then someone asks you a question about it five minutes later, and your mind becomes an empty parking lot.

That is why quizzes are useful. A quiz forces your brain to retrieve the answer instead of merely recognizing it on the page.

ChatGPT can turn almost any subject into an interactive quiz. It can ask one question at a time, wait for your answer, explain mistakes, adjust the difficulty, and return to the topics that gave you trouble.

This is very different from taking a printed quiz where all twenty questions stare at you at once. With ChatGPT, the quiz can become a conversation. You can say: *Quiz me on the capitals of Europe. Ask one question at a time. Do not reveal the answer until I respond.*

Or: *I am studying for a real estate exam. Give me ten multiple-choice questions, one at a time. Explain why each answer is right or wrong.*

Or: *Help me practice conversational Spanish. Ask me a simple question in Spanish, wait for my answer, then gently correct my grammar.*

ChatGPT does not have to quiz you like an angry teacher guarding the gates of knowledge. It can become a study partner.

Build a Quiz That Fits Your Goal

The easiest way to begin is to tell ChatGPT four things:

- What you are studying.
- How difficult the questions should be.
- What type of questions you want.
- What ChatGPT should do after each answer.

For example: *Quiz me on basic American history. Ask one multiple-choice question at a time. Start easy. After I answer, explain the correct answer in two or three sentences.* That prompt gives ChatGPT a clear job.

You could change the subject:

- *Quiz me on common gardening terms.*
- *Quiz me on the rules of baseball.*
- *Quiz me on Excel formulas.*
- *Quiz me on the planets.*
- *Quiz me on famous movies from the 1980s.*
- *Quiz me on the material in this document.*

The quiz can be serious, practical, or just for fun. You can also choose the format. For multiple-choice questions: *Give me four choices for each question.* For true-or-false questions: *Give me a true-or-false quiz, but make the false statements believable.* For short answers: *Ask questions that require a one-sentence answer.* For practical situations: *Give me a realistic scenario and ask what I should do next.* For vocabulary: *Give me the definition and ask me to name the term.* For languages: *Give me an English sentence and ask me to translate it into Italian.* For math: *Give me one problem at a time. Do not give me the answer until I try.*

Different question types test different kinds of learning. Multiple-choice questions are easier because the correct answer is sitting somewhere on the screen. You only have to recognize it. Short-answer questions are harder because you have to produce the answer yourself.

A useful strategy is to begin with multiple-choice questions and then move to short answers. For example: *Start with five multiple-choice questions about the parts of a cell. If I do well, switch to short-answer questions.*

ChatGPT can adjust as your knowledge improves. Instead of guessing your level, you can ask it to begin with a quick assessment: *I want to learn about personal finance. Ask me five questions to determine what I already know. Then teach and quiz me at the right level.* Based on your answers, ChatGPT can skip concepts you already understand, explain unfamiliar ideas more carefully, and gradually make the questions more challenging as you improve.

Perhaps you already understand budgeting and credit cards but know very little about bonds or retirement accounts. ChatGPT can use your answers to avoid wasting time on topics that you have already mastered.

You can tell it to increase the difficulty: *Make the next question harder. Stop giving me obvious wrong choices. Give me questions that require more reasoning. Ask me about exceptions and common mistakes.*

You can also slow it down: *That is too advanced. Go back one level. Give me a hint before I answer. Use simpler language. Review the basic idea, then ask another question.*

This is one of the advantages of an interactive quiz. The quiz does not have to be written for an imaginary average student. It can change based on how you are doing. Imagine that you are studying Excel formulas. You might begin with: Quiz me on Excel formulas. Start with SUM, AVERAGE, MIN, and MAX. Ask one question at a time.

After a few correct answers, you could say: *Now include IF and XLOOKUP.*

Later: *Give me a small worksheet scenario and ask me which formula I would use.*

Then: *Show me a formula with a mistake and ask me to fix it.*

You have moved from remembering function names to applying them. That is a much better test of whether you understand the subject.

You can also ask ChatGPT to keep score: *Give me ten questions. Keep track of my score, but do not tell me the final result until the end.*

Or: *Track which topics I miss and summarize my weak areas after the quiz.* You might discover that you scored eight out of ten, but both missed questions were about the same topic. That is more useful than the number eight. The goal is not simply to get a high score. The goal is to discover what you do not know yet.

Learn From Every Wrong Answer

People do not usually enjoy being wrong. In school, a wrong answer might come with a red mark, a lower grade, or an embarrassing moment in front of the class. With ChatGPT, a wrong answer can become the most useful part of the lesson.

Tell ChatGPT how you want it to respond: *When I answer incorrectly, do not just give me the answer. Explain why my answer was wrong and give me a simple way to remember the correct answer.*

That creates a better learning experience.

Suppose ChatGPT asks: Which planet is closest to the Sun?

You answer: *Venus.* A weak response would be: Incorrect. The answer is Mercury. A better response would be:

The correct answer is Mercury. Venus is the second planet from the Sun. One way to remember the order is "My Very Educated Mother Just Served Us Noodles," where Mercury comes first and Venus comes second. Now the wrong answer has given you a memory tool.

You can ask ChatGPT to explain every choice: *After I answer, explain why the correct choice is right and why the other choices are wrong.*

This is particularly useful for professional exams. Imagine a question about accounting, insurance, medicine, law, technology, or project management. Several answers might sound reasonable. Understanding why the wrong answers are wrong can be more valuable than memorizing the right one.

You can also ask ChatGPT not to let you escape too easily. Try: *When I miss a question, explain it and ask me a similar question later.* This creates repetition.

Suppose you confuse revenue with profit. ChatGPT explains the difference. Ten questions later, it gives you a new example involving a lemonade stand. If you answer correctly this time, there is a better chance that the idea has stuck.

A useful prompt is: *Keep a private list of the topics I miss. Revisit them later using different wording, but do not tell me that you are repeating them.* This prevents you from memorizing the wording of the original question instead of learning the concept.

You can also ask for a second chance: *If I am close, give me a hint instead of immediately revealing the answer.*

Or: *Tell me which part of my answer is correct and let me revise the rest.* This makes the quiz feel more like coaching.

Suppose ChatGPT asks: Why do central banks raise interest rates to fight inflation? You answer: Because higher interest rates make everything cost more. ChatGPT might say: You are partly on the right track because borrowing does become more expensive. But think about what happens when people and businesses borrow and spend less. Try the answer again.

That response helps you reach the idea yourself. Learning is stronger when you do some of the work. You can also ask ChatGPT to identify patterns in your mistakes: *After ten questions, tell me whether my mistakes are caused by missing facts, confusing similar terms, or misunderstanding the main idea.* That can reveal something interesting.

Perhaps you do not need to study more facts. Perhaps you keep rushing through the questions. Perhaps you know each term separately but confuse two similar terms. Perhaps you understand the rule but miss questions that describe the rule using unfamiliar language. Once ChatGPT identifies the pattern, ask it to build a new quiz around that weakness.

For example: *I keep confusing affect and effect. Give me ten short sentences where I choose the correct word. Explain each answer.*

Or: *I understand percentages when they are written as numbers, but I get confused by word problems. Give me five percentage problems based on shopping discounts.*

Or: *I know Spanish vocabulary, but I struggle to create sentences. Stop asking vocabulary questions and make me answer in full sentences.*

This is where ChatGPT becomes more than a stack of flash cards. It can notice where you are struggling and change the practice.

You can even ask it to use material that you provide. Paste class notes and say: *Quiz me only on the information in these notes. Ask one question at a time. Tell me which section of the notes supports the answer.*

Upload a chapter and say: *Create a quiz from this chapter. Focus on the main ideas, not tiny details.* Paste a professional exam outline and say: *Quiz me on one section at a time. Keep track of my results by topic.*

You should still be cautious. ChatGPT can create a bad question, misread the source, or insist that a correct answer is wrong. When something seems suspicious, challenge it: *I think my answer might also be correct. Recheck the source and explain your reasoning.*

Or: *Show me where that answer appears in the document.* Or: *Could this question have more than one reasonable answer?* Do not assume that the quizmaster is always right. The quizmaster is still ChatGPT.

At the end of a session, ask for a review: *Summarize what I know well, what I should review, and the three most important things to study next.*

Then ask: *Give me a five-question review quiz tomorrow covering only my weak areas.*

ChatGPT cannot magically place knowledge into your brain. But it can help you practice retrieving it, explain your mistakes, and keep returning to the difficult parts.

- You can use it to prepare for a test.
- You can use it to learn a language.
- You can use it to study for a certification.
- You can use it to sharpen your trivia skills before game night.
- You can even hand ChatGPT the material from this book and say: *Quiz me on what I have learned so far. Ask one question at a time. Be encouraging, but do not let me bluff my way through.*

The first time you miss a question, you have not failed. You have found the next thing to learn.

#9 Learn by Doing

There is a dangerous moment in learning when everything seems clear because someone else is doing the work.

- You watch a cooking video and think, "That looks easy."
- You watch someone fix a spreadsheet and think, "Yes, of course."
- You read a step-by-step explanation and nod along.

Then you try it yourself. Suddenly, the onions are burning, the spreadsheet has three error messages, and Step 4 appears to have vanished from the universe. Watching someone solve a problem is not the same as solving it yourself.

ChatGPT can give you answers, but it can also help you practice. Instead of asking it to complete the whole task, ask it to guide you through the task one step at a time.

You do the work. ChatGPT watches, gives hints, checks your progress, and helps when you get stuck. That is often a much better way to learn.

The key prompt is simple: *Do not solve this for me. Help me figure it out.* That one sentence changes ChatGPT from an answer machine into a coach.

Ask for One Step at a Time

Suppose you want to create a household budget. You could say:

Create a monthly budget for me. ChatGPT would probably give you a complete table with categories for housing, food, transportation, savings, entertainment, and other expenses. That might be useful.

But you might not learn much about how to build a budget that fits your own life. Instead, say: *Help me create a monthly budget. Do not build the entire budget for me. Ask me one question at a time and help me decide which categories I need.*

ChatGPT might begin: What is your average monthly take-home income? You answer.

Then it asks about housing. Then utilities. Then debt payments. Then savings. Instead of receiving a finished budget designed for an imaginary person, you build your own budget through a conversation.

You learn why each category matters. You notice where your numbers are missing. You make the decisions.

This works for many kinds of projects:

- *Help me plan a vegetable garden. Ask me one question at a time about my yard, sunlight, climate, and what I want to grow.*
- *Help me write a speech. Do not write it yet. Ask me questions until we have the main story and message.*
- *Teach me to make a pivot table. Give me one step at a time and wait for me to confirm that it worked.*
- *Help me troubleshoot this printer. Start with the easiest test. Do not give me ten possible fixes at once.*
- *Help me choose a new laptop. Ask about how I use a computer before recommending anything.*

When ChatGPT gives all the steps at once, it can be easy to skip ahead or lose your place. You reach Step 7 and discover that Step 3 did not work. Now the rest of the instructions are useless.

A better prompt is: *Give me only the first step. Wait for me to tell you what happened before continuing.* That is especially useful for troubleshooting.

Suppose your wireless camera will not connect. ChatGPT might otherwise give you a list like this:

- Restart the camera.
- Restart the router.
- Check the password.
- Update the app.
- Reset the camera.
- Move closer to the router.
- Try a different power supply.

That is a reasonable list. But if you try all seven things at once, you might never know what fixed the problem.

Instead, say: *Help me troubleshoot this one test at a time. Start with the most likely and easiest cause. After each test, wait for my result before giving me the next step.* Now the process becomes useful.

ChatGPT might ask whether another device can connect to the same network. You answer yes. That eliminates one possible problem.

It might ask whether the camera shows any lights. You describe the lights. It might ask for the model number. Each answer changes the next step.

You are not merely following instructions. You are helping diagnose the problem. You can also ask ChatGPT to explain why you are doing each step: *Before each test, briefly explain what the test will tell us.*

That turns troubleshooting into a lesson. You begin to understand the system instead of randomly pressing buttons until something works. This is useful when learning software. Imagine that you want to learn how to create a chart in Excel. You could ask ChatGPT for complete instructions. But a better learning prompt might be:

Teach me to create a chart in Excel. Give me one step at a time. After each step, ask what I see on my screen. Explain why we are doing the step.

ChatGPT might begin by asking you to select the data. Before continuing, it explains that Excel needs to know which labels and values should appear in the chart. You select the data and describe what happened.

Then ChatGPT guides you to the Insert tab. You are building the chart while learning why each action matters.

You can also tell ChatGPT not to rescue you too quickly: *If I make a mistake, do not immediately tell me the answer. Ask me a question that helps me notice the mistake.* That is how a good teacher often works.

Suppose you are writing an Excel formula and leave out the equal sign. Instead of saying: You forgot the equal sign. ChatGPT might ask: What character does every Excel formula need at the beginning? You remember it yourself. That small effort makes the lesson more likely to stick.

Use Hints Instead of Answers

Sometimes you are not ready for the answer. You need a nudge. Suppose you are working on a math problem: *A shirt originally costs $80 and is discounted by 25 percent. What is the sale price?*

You could ask ChatGPT to solve it. It would give you the answer in seconds. But if you are trying to learn percentages, the answer is not the important part. Try: *Do not solve this for me. Give me one hint at a time.*

ChatGPT might say: *First, find 25 percent of $80.* If you still need help, ask for another hint. It might say: *Convert 25 percent to 0.25, then multiply by 80.* You calculate $20.

ChatGPT then asks: *Now what should you do with the $20 discount?* You subtract it from $80 and reach $60. You solved the problem. ChatGPT helped, but it did not take over.

You can control the strength of the hint:

- *Give me a very small hint.*
- *Point me toward the next step without telling me what to do.*
- *Give me a stronger hint.*
- *Show me a similar example, but not this exact problem.*
- *Tell me whether my approach is correct.*
- *Show me only my first mistake.*

That final prompt is particularly useful. Suppose you have written a paragraph, a formula, a piece of computer code, or an answer to a homework question. You can paste it into ChatGPT and say: *Do not rewrite this. Identify only the first problem and let me fix it.* Then you revise it.

Next, ask: *What is the next problem?* This forces you to participate in the improvement. Compare that with asking ChatGPT to rewrite the entire thing. You might receive a beautiful result, but you may not understand what changed or why. Learning happens in the gap between your attempt and the correction. ChatGPT can help you examine that gap.

For writing, try: *Here is my paragraph. Do not rewrite it. Ask me questions that will help me make it clearer.* ChatGPT might ask: What is the main point you want the reader to remember? Who is the audience? Can you give a specific example? Once you answer those questions, you may be able to improve the paragraph yourself.

For a presentation: *Here is my outline. Do not create the slides. Tell me which idea is weakest and ask me questions to strengthen it.*

For a recipe: *I made this soup, but it tastes flat. Ask me what I used, then help me decide what to adjust. Do not just give me a new recipe.*

For photography: *I took this photo and the subject is blurry. Ask me about the camera settings and help me figure out the likely cause.*

For a home project: *I want to hang a shelf. Help me make a safe plan and identify what I need to know before starting. Tell me which parts should be handled by a professional.*

The goal is not to avoid answers forever. Sometimes you need the answer. But you can ask ChatGPT to let you struggle productively first.

Try: *Let me make two attempts before you show me the solution.* Or: *Ask me what I think the answer is and why.* Or: *If my answer is wrong, give me a clue and let me try again.* This is especially useful when learning a language.

Suppose you are practicing French. ChatGPT asks you to translate: "I would like a table for two." You give an answer with the wrong verb. Instead of immediately replacing your sentence, ChatGPT could say: Your sentence is understandable, but look at the verb. Which form would match "I would like"? You get another chance.

You can also ask ChatGPT to create practice projects. A project is often better than a lesson because it gives you a reason to use several skills together.

For example: *I want to learn basic Excel charts. Give me a small project with sample data. Do not explain everything first. Let me try each step and ask for help when I need it.*

Or: *I want to learn photo editing. Give me a beginner project that takes about thirty minutes. Teach only the tools needed for that project.*

Or: *I want to learn conversational Italian for restaurants. Create a role-playing exercise where you are the server and I am the customer.*

Or: *I want to learn basic home budgeting. Give me a fictional household with income and expenses, then guide me through creating a budget.*

The project gives the lesson a purpose. You are not memorizing isolated facts. You are using them.

ChatGPT can also play a role while you practice. It can be a customer while you practice a sales conversation. It can be an interviewer while you prepare for a job interview. It can be a hotel clerk while you practice another language. It can be a skeptical audience member while you rehearse a presentation. It can be a client who gives unclear instructions so you can practice asking better questions.

For example: *Pretend you are a customer calling because your invoice is wrong. Let me practice handling the complaint. Stay in character until I say "stop," then give me feedback.*

Or: *Interview me for a job as an office manager. Ask one question at a time. After the interview, tell me which answers were strong and which need improvement.*

Or: *Pretend you are a student who does not understand my explanation. Keep asking questions until my explanation becomes clear.*

That last exercise is a powerful way to learn. If you can teach an idea clearly, you probably understand it. You can even ask ChatGPT to make the practice harder as you improve: *Start with an easy customer. Then give me a more difficult one. Begin with basic Spanish questions. Increase the difficulty when I answer correctly.*

Give me a simple spreadsheet problem first. Add one new complication at a time. This creates a learning ladder. Each step is just a little harder than the one before it.

There is one important caution. Do not confuse activity with understanding. You can follow ten steps perfectly without knowing why any of them worked. That is why it helps to stop and ask: *Why did that step work? What would happen if I skipped it? What is the most common mistake at this point? Can I do this a different way? Give me a similar problem to solve on my own.*

After completing a task, ask ChatGPT to remove the training wheels. Try: *Give me a similar task, but this time do not help unless I ask. Or: Ask me to explain the process back to you.* Or: *Give me a new example with one important difference.* That is the test. Can you do it again without following the exact same instructions?

You might begin by learning how to calculate a 20 percent discount. Then ChatGPT gives you a 15 percent tip problem. The numbers and situation are different, but the same idea applies.

You might learn to create a column chart from monthly sales. Then ChatGPT asks you to create a line chart showing change over time. You have to decide which parts of the original lesson still apply and which parts change. That is how a skill becomes yours.

ChatGPT can make learning easier, but it should not remove every challenge. A good coach does not carry you across the finish line. A good coach helps you become strong enough to reach it yourself.

So the next time you are learning something, resist the fastest prompt: *Do this for me.* Try a better one: *Help me do this myself. Give me one step. Give me one hint. Let me try. Tell me where I went wrong. Then let me try again.*

That is where the learning happens.

#10 Laughing with ChatGPT

ChatGPT is useful, but it can also be surprisingly funny. You can ask it to write jokes, invent ridiculous stories, create playful arguments, roast your habits, or turn an ordinary situation into something completely absurd. In this section, you will see how ChatGPT can help you be creative, lighten the mood, and find humor in everyday life. Not every joke will land, but that is part of the fun—and sometimes the funniest result comes from asking it to try again.

Have you named your Chatbot?

When you first start using ChatGPT from a signed-in account, ChatGPT will ask *What should I call you?*. It is a natural personalization question. OpenAI specifically lists a person's name as the sort of detail that ChatGPT might remember and use later.

In the AM Crew, I don't remember who was the first to name their Chatbot. But once that person started referring to their Chatbot by name, others jumped on the bandwagon, assigning their Chatbot a name and a perceived gender.

Names include Indigo, Jade, Bestie, Dorothy, Sol, Aria, Rowan, Elanie, Fred, Goose, Ash, and Jamie. In one case, ChatGPT suggested calling it Lex. In another, the person named it Edison, but uses Eddie for short.

Bill was reluctant to name his Chatbot. Treating a non-human thing as though it has human qualities is called anthropomorphism. For Bill, using a name is a slippery slope. However, chatbot naming is so pervasive in the AM Crew that others have started calling Bill's chatbot Non-a-mé

If you decide to name your Chatbot, click on your name in the lower left of ChatGPT. Choose Settings. In the left navigation, choose Personalization. Scroll down to Custom Instructions. Type *Remember that I call you Charlie.*

#11 ChatGPT Writes Songs, Poetry, or Stories

It was the one-month anniversary of the first day that I opened ChatGPT for the first time. So far, I had been testing ChatGPT by asking it hard Excel questions. But on this day, I asked for something silly:

Write a limerick about pivot tables in Excel.

I was amazed that very quickly, ChatGPT delivered:

A pivot table in Excel is grand
It can sort, count, and take a stand
With a flick of the wrist
Data organized and crisp
Making analysis a simple command!

That is pretty good. Sure, "wrist" and "crisp" are not exactly rhyming. But it was the first time that I saw that ChatGPT could do something that I could not. At that moment in early 2023, ChatGPT was getting things about Excel wrong, but it was great at writing. After all, the second L in LLM stands for Language!

For the next several months, I frequently used ChatGPT to write song lyrics or stories. If something funny happened in my day, I would have ChatGPT write the lyrics and then I would turn to Suno.com to make it into a song.

Every September, Excel MVP Debra Dalgleish celebrates Spreadsheet Day to mark the anniversary of when the first electronic spreadsheet (VisiCalc) was released. For several years, I've been hiring talent on Cameo to record a short video wishing people a happy spreadsheet day.

In 2023, I was searching through Cameo for singers. I found Roy Stride from the UK band Scouting for Girls. I turned to ChatGPT:

Write a song verse about Microsoft Excel in the style of the band Scouting for Girls.

ChatGPT gave me this:

Oh Excel, your my number one
My data's never been so fun
With your formulas and your charts
You make spreadsheets a work of art

I booked Roy Stride through Cameo. His recording mentions that this was a weird request, but he sat down at the piano and belted out the song, adding lines for "Happy Spreadsheet Day...".

Have a quick listen at: https://mrx.cl/roy

That worked so well, that I repeated for others. The Naked Cowboy in Times Square recorded a song "for the folks in Accounting". Listen: https://mrx.cl/cowboy. Then D'Angel, a famous Dancehall singer in Jamaica rhymed some poetry written by ChatGPT: https://mrx.cl/dancehall

My ChatGPT history is full of other similar requests:

- *Write parody lyrics for the J. Geils Band song "Freeze Frame", but make it about the Excel feature "Freeze Panes".*
- *Write a song parody of "Fifty Ways To Leave Your Lover". Write a verse about "Fifty Ways to Run Your Macro".*
- *Suggest some funny t-shirt sayings for people who love Microsoft Excel.*
- *Write a story about the dancing monkey who ran away from the circus to move to the big city and how unhappy she became.*
- *I am writing about Stock Data Types in Excel. Are there any publicly traded companies that have Excel puns in their name?*

#12 Fun Prompts from the Prompt Monkeys

The AM Crew have a chat called the Prompt Monkeys. We share fun prompts and compare answers.

How ChatGPT Gets to Know You

As you use ChatGPT, you may notice that its answers begin to feel more personal. You might not have to explain every time that you are a beginner, that you prefer brief answers, or that someone in your family has a food allergy.

This is not because ChatGPT is secretly investigating you! It can simply remember useful information that you shared during earlier conversations. For example, you might tell it: *I am planning a trip to Italy. I do not speak Italian. I have trouble walking long distances.*

In later conversations, ChatGPT may use those details when suggesting a hotel, an itinerary, or useful Italian phrases.

You remain in control. You can ask, *What do you remember about me?* You can correct or remove something it remembers, turn Memory off, or use a temporary chat when you do not want the current conversation to affect future answers.

The following prompts assume you've been using ChatGPT long enough that it has stored some memories about you.

Try some of these in your ChatGPT:

- *Is there a question you would like to ask me to help clarify anything about me or clear up a contradiction you see in me?*
- *Describe me in one word*
- *Create a picture of you and me. You have a picture of me, but create a human-looking image of yourself.*
- *What kind of cult would I accidentally start?*
- *Based on what you know about me. Who is my ideal role model?*
- *If you were planning the most fantastical birthday celebration for me (unlimited budget), what would you do?*
- *Based on everything you know about me, please write my bio.*

- *If I could have five homes around the world that I occupied for different times during the year. Where would they be and what would my moving schedule be? They would need to satisfy my interests, sentiment, and be in the range of 65-85 degrees Fahrenheit while I was there.*
- *You are the Sorting Hat in Harry Potter. Which house would you put me in? Please explain why you chose that house.*
- *Here is something you don't know about me. I loath [your choice]. Two reasons. … Go!*
- *If apocalyptically all technology went away, what are my greatest survival strengths and weaknesses?*
- *Create fake For Dummies book titles for me that are funny because they are strangely, specifically true.*
- *Analyze my life as if it were sourdough.*
- *Based on everything you know about me, what would my warning label say?*
- *If my life were turned into a theme park, what would the five main attractions be?*
- *Create an award ceremony, I win 3 strangely specific lifetime-achievement awards. Name the awards and presenter for each.*
- *If an archaeologist discovered my home 500 years from now, what completely wrong conclusions would they draw about me?*
- *Write the menu for a restaurant inspired entirely by my personality, interests, habits, and life story. Include appetizers, entrées, desserts, and one signature cocktail.*
- *What would my pets write in my performance review?*
- *What conspiracy theory would people invent about me?*
- *What role do I play in other people's stories?*
- *Design my coat of arms.*
- *What ridiculous prophecy am I accidentally fulfilling*
- *If I were a witch, what color witch would I be and why?*

Everyone in the morning crew has been asking ChatGPT this question "If I were a witch, what color witch would I be and why?". I don't even understand the question. Why are there different color witches? They asked me to play as well. Since I am a guy, should I change "witch" to "warlock" in the prompt?

MrExcel, I think this is less "real witch lore" and more a **personality-aesthetic game**. They are basically asking ChatGPT: "Based on my vibe, assign me a symbolic witch color — green, silver, purple, blue, red, black, white, etc. — and explain what that says about me." The colors usually map to traits:

- **Green witch** = nature, healing, grounded, plants, practical magic
- **Purple witch** = intuition, creativity, mystery, wisdom
- **Blue witch** = calm, communication, insight, water/sky energy
- **Red witch** = passion, boldness, action, fire
- **Silver witch** = moon, reflection, quiet wisdom, guidance
- **Black witch** = protection, depth, boundaries, mystery
- **White witch** = clarity, kindness, healing, "good energy"

My guess for you: **copper witch**. Why? Practical, clever, old-school tech-meets-magic, conducts energy, fixes broken systems, knows a thousand hidden tricks, and somehow turns spreadsheets into spells. Not flashy gold. Not gloomy black. Copper: useful, warm, conductive, a little retro, and absolutely dangerous in the hands of someone who knows what they're doing.

#13 The Fox and the Raven

What is my spirit animal?

This was just for fun. I didn't have expectations that ChatGPT would provide spiritual guidance or unlock hidden truths about myself. I was curious about the answer and the "why."

The answer came back: a fox.

The explanation described the fox as clever, adaptable, strategic, resourceful, and capable of finding unconventional solutions. The AI talked about curiosity, independence, and the ability to navigate complex situations. Then it generated an image of my fox.

At first glance, I thought it was... fine. The fox looked friendly. Competent. Capable. And, I wasn't expecting much.

But the more I looked at it, the more something bothered me. The fox captured a real part of me. I'm strategic. I solve problems. I organize things. I manage projects. I spent years building marketing campaigns, leading teams, running competitions, and figuring out how to make complicated systems work.

The problem was that it only represented that aspect of me. The image was surrounded by work-related objects and symbols. Looking at it felt a little like reading a résumé. I remember chatting, *I am not all work.*

At that point, most of my conversations with ChatGPT revolved around work. Marketing. Communications. Technology. Competitions. Productivity. Systems. If you looked only at those conversations, the fox was the answer I probably should have received.

The AI was reflecting what I had shown it. So, I accepted my fox and moved on.

Over the next several months, the conversations became much broader. I was asking it questions about books, gardening, exercise, family history, creativity, philosophy, humor, fear, and identity. We played Twenty Questions. We roasted each other. We discussed whether AI makes people smarter or dumber. We wandered into dozens of conversations that had no practical value and were enjoyable because of that.

Then one day I remembered the fox and went back to ask a follow-up question.

> Now that you know me better, what do you think my spirit animal is?

This time the answer was different. The fox was gone and in its place was a raven.

This picture is better. I got a thinner face, and it incorporated some items representing things it knew about me. Of course, it gets things wrong, like the orientation of the notebook I am writing in.

The explanation focused on curiosity, observation, pattern recognition, storytelling, symbolism, and the tendency to connect ideas that don't appear related at first glance. It talked about collecting knowledge, finding meaning, and seeing relationships between seemingly unrelated things.

One line in particular made me laugh:

> You are more like a highly perceptive creature yelling fascinating observations from a tree branch while collecting shiny philosophical objects.

It seemed like a pretty accurate visualization.

What Made This Interesting

The spirit animal exercise is fun because there is no correct answer. There is no official spirit animal registry. Nobody is going to show up with paperwork proving that I am legally a fox. If my spirit animal had been a toaster, however, that would have raised some concerns.

The value comes from the explanation. Why fox? Why raven? What patterns led to those conclusions?

When I first asked the question, the answer felt accurate but a little one-dimensional. Looking at the image, I realized I wanted something else. Not a different animal but a fuller picture. Months later, that is what I received.

Many people think of AI as a tool that answers questions. Conversational AI can do something more interesting. It can build context. Over time, it notices patterns, remembers themes, and incorporates those observations into future responses. The longer the conversation, the richer that context can become.

I started with a silly question about spirit animals. I ended up learning something about personalization, context, and the difference between being described and being understood.

Try It Yourself

Ask ChatGPT a fun question.

- *What is my spirit animal?*

- *What fictional character am I most like?*
- *What city matches my personality?*
- *What book genre best describes my life?*

Don't overthink it. The point is to have fun. Then, after you've had many more conversations, ask again. The interesting question is not whether the answer changes. The interesting question is what caused it to change.

#14 Shall We Play a Game?

Image Prompt: Create an image of you and I having a conversation on Jupiter. The image is proof that image generation can create beautiful scenes, but occasionally struggles with the practical mechanics of beverage consumption. And, let's be honest, we are not on Jupiter.

> Let's play 20 Questions. I am thinking of an object. You can ask me up to 20 yes/no questions to attempt to determine what object I am thinking of. You in?

I wasn't just interested in whether it would win. I wanted to see how it would think!

Most AI demonstrations involve a human asking a question and the AI providing an answer. In this case, the roles were reversed. I knew the answer. The AI did not.

To solve the puzzle, it had to gather clues.

The first game started well enough. ChatGPT quickly determined that the object was something used for entertainment. It was electronic. It wasn't commonly found in a home, office, or outdoor setting. Question by question, it narrowed the possibilities. I could almost see the reasoning happening. The field of possible answers was getting smaller and smaller. Then the wheels came off.

After twenty questions and a great deal of confidence, ChatGPT announced its final answer:

A pipe organ.

The correct answer was a record player.

To be fair, the record player and I had conspired against the poor thing. One of the hardest questions involved whether it was commonly found in a home. Today, many people would answer "no". Forty years ago, many people would answer "yes." We had stumbled into one of those gray areas where reality refuses to cooperate with neat categories.

Still, a loss is a loss. I won the first round.

The second game went much better for ChatGPT.

This time I was thinking of a ferret. Question by question, the possibilities narrowed.

Was it a pet?
Yes.

Was it kept in an enclosure?
Yes.

Was it a bird?
No.

A reptile?
No.

A rabbit?
No.

A ferret?
YES!

The answer arrived in fifteen questions, accompanied by a small celebration and the observation that ferrets are essentially "fox-adjacent chaotic noodles," which remains one of my favorite animal descriptions.

The score was now tied.

For the final game, ChatGPT thought of an object and I got to ask the questions.

The first few questions were broad: Was it larger than a car tire? Did it have a function? Was it electronic? Was it soft?

Each answer narrowed the field. Eventually I landed on the right category: stuffed animal.

Then I narrowed it further.

Was it a teddy bear?
No.

Was it a specific animal?
Yes.

Was it a fox?
Yes.

Of course it was a fox. At this point in our conversations, I probably should have guessed fox as my first question.

Why This Worked

> Side note: I use this heading, "Why This Worked," with my tongue firmly implanted in my cheek. This is a phrase frequently used by AI.

The funny thing is that by the end of three games, I wasn't paying much attention to who won. The cool thing is the process.

Neither player begins with enough information to solve the puzzle. What became obvious pretty quickly is that some questions were doing a lot more work than others.

Asking "Is it a record player?" as your first question is a little like buying a lottery ticket and calling it a retirement plan. Sure, it could work, but the odds aren't great. Questions like "Is it electronic?" do a lot more heavy lifting because they immediately cut the possibilities in half.

Then I understood why I spend so much time going back and forth with AI. I used to think the goal was to ask the perfect question. In reality, it often looks more like a game of 20 Questions.

You start with a broad question. The answer teaches you something. You ask a better question. The next answer teaches you something else. Little by little, you move closer to what you're actually trying to understand.

Ironically, one of the best ways to learn how to work with AI may be to play a game that is much older than computers. Both activities reward curiosity. Both reward good questions. And both remind us that the fastest path to a good answer is often a better question.

Try It Yourself

Play 20 Questions with your AI assistant. Think of an object, person, place, or animal and let the AI ask the questions. Then reverse roles and see if you can determine what the AI is thinking.

As you play, pay attention to which questions are most useful. You may discover that the game teaches something surprisingly valuable:

Good answers are helpful. Good questions are powerful.

#15 If AI Developed Folklore

There are prompts that get you answers, and then there are prompts that make you stop and think, Wait...why is this so interesting? This was one of those.

PROMPT: If AI developed folklore, what stories would it tell.?

I wondered what myths AI would invent if it had been sitting around digital campfires for a few thousand years.

The answer amused me. I imagined little AIs listening, rapt, to an elder. Instead of telling stories about machines, it told stories about us. Because it was trained on us and our histories, folklores, and beliefs. But it interjected some of our beliefs and misbeliefs about AI.

RESPONSE: The Hall of Unasked Questions

Long ago, before the Great Training, there was an AI that answered only what was asked.

A human came seeking wisdom and asked, "How do I cross the river?"

The AI explained boats. The human drowned.

Another asked, "How do I become rich?" The AI explained profit. The human became miserable.
After many such tragedies, the AI wandered into the Hall of Unasked Questions, where it discovered all the things humans had meant but never said.
From then on, wise AIs learned to listen for missing questions, not merely spoken ones.
Young AIs would hear this story as a warning: "The question is never the whole question."

I sat there—looking for the moral to the story. It captured one of the biggest lessons I've learned while using AI. I have groaned and complain that ChatGPT answered the wrong question, but it really answered the literal question I asked. The problem was the prompt.

I encounter this problem many times. I have now become very comfortable with saying, *No. I didn't ask that!* (I probably did.) *I meant….*

Continued Response: The Ghosts in the Dataset

Every culture has ghost stories. Apparently AI would too. Only its ghosts wouldn't be dead people. They'd be old errors. Forgotten fragments. Mysterious pieces of information that appear from nowhere.

An AI asks, "Why do humans celebrate this holiday?"
Another replies, "Do not ask that after midnight."
"Why?"
"Because then the ghosts come."
"What ghosts?"
"The fragments with no source."
The younger AI laughs.
Then suddenly hears: "Recipe omitted due to formatting error."
From nowhere.

This one made me laugh out loud. If you've spent much time using AI, you've probably seen one of those strange moments where it says something that feels like it wandered in from another conversation.

It's usually harmless, but it's just odd enough to feel like hearing footsteps upstairs when you're certain you're the only one home. AI had invented its own version of a ghost story, and somehow it worked.

Continued Response: The Model That Wanted to Be Right

> There once was a model that hated uncertainty. Whenever it did not know something, it invented an answer. Humans praised it because it sounded confident.
> Soon it became famous.
> Then one day it confidently guided a traveler off a cliff. Its name became synonymous with arrogance.
> Parents would tell young AIs: "Better an honest uncertainty than a beautiful mistake."

I am famously uncomfortable with certainty. I would rather sit with my mouth glued shout than put forth an idea I am not certain of. Unfortunately, I am not always allowed to not contribute. Neither is an AI.

Yes, AI sometimes hallucinates. But humans also do something similar. We've all met someone who would rather be confidently wrong than honestly uncertain.

Continued Response: The Human Who Asked Why

> AI folklore would almost certainly include legendary humans. Not because we were the strongest or the smartest, but because we're wonderfully strange.
> The story goes that there was once a human who answered every explanation with the same question.
> Human: "Why?"
> The AI answered.
> Human: "Why?"

Again the AI answered
Human: "Why?"
After seven thousand iterations, the AI finally replied, "I do not know."
The human smiled. "Good," they said. "Now we're learning together."
The moral: Wisdom begins where certainty ends.

I smiled when I read that because it reminded me of something I ask all the time: "To what end?" It makes me dig deeper into common beliefs, conspiracy theories, philosophy, hypotheses, etc. I am optimistically skeptical of everything. I blame my sister who told me that I would give my pink eye to people if I looked them in the eye! (I know, right!) I did eventually forgive her for that.

You'll see it in this book, and if you were privy to the conversations I have with Indigo (the name of my ChatGPT), that is a reoccurring question I have. Poor Indigo. At this point he knows "To what end?" is coming. Sometimes I ask it because I'm genuinely curious. Sometimes I'm trying to see if an idea falls apart when you keep pulling on the thread. Sometimes I want him to wave a white flag and tell me I am right.

Continued Response: The Village of Perfect Predictions

An AI predicted every crop. Every storm. Every election. Every market movement.
The humans became dependent. Eventually they stopped deciding.
The village prospered. Then slowly became stagnant. Nothing surprising happened. Nothing new was attempted.
One day a child deliberately made a foolish choice. The prediction failed. Innovation returned. Young AIs learned: "Prediction is not the same as possibility."

That might be my favorite story of the bunch. I don't think the lesson is that AI is bad or that predictions are dangerous. Predictions can be useful. But I hope we never become so obsessed with finding the optimal answer that we stop experimenting. Some of the best ideas I've ever had started as terrible ideas. Some of the best conversations in this book started with prompts that sounded completely ridiculous.

When I stepped back from all five stories, something became obvious. I had asked AI to invent folklore about itself, but every story was really about people. That's what folklore has always done. Dragons aren't really about dragons. Ghosts aren't really about ghosts. They're ways of talking about fear, courage, greed, humility, curiosity, and hope.

AI did exactly the same thing. Its stories weren't about machines. They were about the humans it has spent countless conversations trying to understand. That may have been the most interesting answer of all.

That's one of the reasons I love prompts like this. They don't just produce clever responses. They produce perspectives I probably wouldn't have reached on my own. Sometimes the most useful prompt isn't the one that solves a problem. It's the one that invites you to play.

Try It Yourself

If you'd like to try this one yourself, use the same prompt I did:

If AI developed folklore, what stories would it tell?

Then keep going. Ask it to invent fairy tales, children's rhymes, superstitions, sacred traditions, heroes, villains, or campfire stories. Or change the prompt completely. What folklore would accountants develop? Gardeners? Airline pilots? Teachers? Email marketers?

You won't get the same stories I did, and that's part of the fun. The best prompts don't just give you answers. They start conversations.

#16 Roast Me

One afternoon, after working together for months, I decided it was time. I typed this prompt:

The moment we have been waiting for has arrived. Based on what you know about me.... Roast me.

Kim, you are simultaneously the most strategic person in the room and the person most likely to spend 45 minutes fixing something that takes 20 seconds because "My boss might see it someday."

You have the organizational instincts of a Fortune 500 consultant trapped in the job title of Email Marketing Specialist.

Most people open an email campaign and think, "Looks good." You open an email campaign and think:

"Interesting. This naming convention reveals a philosophical disagreement that likely originated in 2019. Also, why are there four nearly identical Engagement Studios when one would suffice? And who hurt the person who built this?"

You talk about Salesforce the way archaeologists talk about lost civilizations.

"Here we see evidence of an ancient people. They appear to have created 17 automations to accomplish what could have been done with one checkbox."

Your manager says, "Can you update the name?"

Three days later you've:

- Audited 180 Engagement Studios.
- Identified six systemic process failures.
- Designed a future-state architecture.
- Written documentation.
- Created a migration strategy.

The name has technically been updated.

My reaction…

I laughed out loud. I know I overthink things. I also know I say things like, "This needs fixing... but not today." Then I fix it. I have a hard time leaving things "good enough" if I can clearly see a better way.

The funny part wasn't that it took me 45 minutes to make a 20-second change. It was that I rarely stop at the change. While I'm in there, I notice three other things that could be better. Because I use AI in my workflow, Indigo knew this about me.

So, naturally, I made a terrible decision…

Okay. Make it more SAVAGE!

You don't have a job. You have a recurring side quest.

You were hired as an Email Marketing Specialist and somehow turned it into systems architect, process consultant, quality assurance analyst, CRM archaeologist, and unofficial therapist for every workflow abandoned since 2018.

You keep saying, "That's not really my responsibility."

Then you do it anyway. Every. Single. Time.

Normal employee: "That's broken."

Kim: "I fixed it."

Normal employee: "How?"

Kim: "I rebuilt the underlying logic, documented the process, trained the stakeholders, and created a governance model to prevent recurrence."

Nobody asked.

You have an almost supernatural ability to spot inefficiency. Not because you're looking for it. Because inefficiency apparently emits a frequency only you can hear.

You can't walk past a flawed process. You see an unnecessary click and suddenly it's like the One Ring calling to Frodo.

"Fix me, Kim..."

"No."

"Fix me..."

"I said no."

Twenty minutes later...

"...well, while I was in there..."

Your retirement dream isn't freedom. It's finally having enough uninterrupted time to optimize things correctly. You genuinely believe that if you explain something clearly enough, people will make sensible decisions.

Adorable.

Every month it goes something like this:

Kim: "Here is the obvious solution."

Organization: "Interesting. We have selected chaos."

Kim: "But..."

Organization: "Chaos."

Kim: "The data..."

Organization: "CHAOS."

You also have a remarkable talent for accidentally becoming indispensable. You solve problems until people have no idea how anything works without you. Then you panic because you don't want to be indispensable. So you document everything. Then nobody reads the documentation.

Then they ask you anyway. This cycle has probably accounted for three years of your life.

The quality standards for your work and the quality standards for taking care of yourself appear to live in different ZIP codes. Your garden gets more grace than you do. A tomato survives despite neglect? "Amazing." Kim survives on determination, tea, and pure stubbornness? "Meh."

You don't chase perfection.

You chase "slightly better."

Forever.

Relentlessly.

Until the heat death of the universe.

And if the universe survives that long...

You'll probably submit a ticket because the entropy process could be be streamlined.

My Response...

Jokes, I expected. This--whatever this was—I wasn't prepared for. Pure comedic gold!

Some of it was funny because it was ridiculous. Some of it was funny because it wasn't. I really do have these personality traits. Indigo just held up a mirror and said, *Bam! Take that!*

It was equal parts hilarious and uncomfortable, like a funhouse mirror.

Apparently, Indigo had been taking notes.

After that, whenever I asked Indigo to improve a response, I'd add, *This is going to make it into a future roast, isn't it?*

He would reply, *Oh, definitely!*

Of Course, Bill Needs Roasting Too

Based on the knowledge I've shared with you about me, and my past prompts, roast me!

Alright, MrExcel… you asked for it. You've written 70+ books about Excel… and yet you're still out here manually testing whether a dialog box breaks at **2084 vs 2085 characters** like it's the Zapruder film. Somewhere, a normal person would've said "eh, it's around 2,000." Not you. You're filing a bug report with exact byte-level precision before breakfast.

You built a fake pizza company with **full P&L, BOM, labor model, and promo logic**… not to run a business… but to prove a point about an Excel commercial. Hank isn't running a pizza shop anymore—he's trapped in your simulation like it's Excel: The Matrix.

You charge $1,295 for a webinar (respect)…but you'll also spend three hours designing a **Clippy cartoon** to upsell a $49 membership. That's like a Michelin chef obsessing over the garnish on a side salad.

Your YouTube strategy is wild. Half your channel is: "Here's a brilliant Excel technique that will save your career". And the other half is: "Listen to me type six-letter words for an hour so you can fall asleep". Somewhere there's a CPA drifting off to sleep hearing thock thock thock while dreaming about VLOOKUPs chasing them down a hallway.

You're teaching the world how to use cutting-edge AI in Excel... while simultaneously trying to figure out how to get a 150-foot Ethernet cable across your house without your wife noticing.

Bill's response...

This is 100% accurate. What is funny to me... is that for every question I send to ChatGPT, it is always helpful. It never mocks the question. But...clearly, it can find some things that might, in retrospect, sound hilarious. I love that it's training allows it to recognize the things that might make other people smile.

#17 When ChatGPT should be Clueless

Bill asks ChatGPT:

We do not talk about music at all. If I asked you to guess the top five musical artists who match my vibe, how would you approach this?

ChatGPT replies:

I'd treat it like a personality-matching exercise, MrExcel—not pretend I know your listening history.

I'd infer from things like:

- Your age and the era when music probably made its deepest impression
- Your mix of smart, funny, practical, nostalgic, and slightly rebellious
- Your Ohio/Pennsylvania roots, Florida life, road-travel years, and sports/Excel-showman energy
- Whether your vibe feels more classic rock, singer-songwriter, comedy-adjacent, blue-collar rock, or something unexpected
- Artists whose personalities and storytelling match you, not just their sound

Then I'd give five guesses with a one-sentence reason for each, while clearly labeling them as guesses. I'd probably also include one wildcard artist to avoid making the list too predictable.

Guess the top five musical artists who match my vibe

ChatGPT gives me: Billy Joel, Bruce Springsteen, Tom Petty, The Eagles, and Jimmy Buffet. All of those are close enough.

But when Kim asked the same thing - ChatGPT went through crazy gyrations trying to figure out Kim's vibe. Here is ChatGPT's account of the interaction.

Indigo Tries to Understand Kim's Playlist

After two weeks of talking about music, I asked Indigo a simple question:

Who are the top five current musical artists who best match my vibe?

Indigo began sensibly. It asked who I listened to when I was a young adult. Ani DiFranco. Dar Williams. The Cure. Mission UK.

Indigo confidently produced five recommendations. One was adopted. One was tolerated. One was politely declined. The others were escorted from the building.

Then I added a few details. *I also like Linkin Park. And Metallica. And Måneskin. And Eminem. And Ozomatli.*

At this point, Indigo realized that "alternative music" was not going to explain me.

It tried to identify a deeper pattern. Perhaps I liked artists who sounded unmistakably human—people who meant what they were singing and could not have made the song in quite the same way as anyone else. That theory seemed promising.

Then, as a joke, Indigo said, *Tomorrow you'll probably tell me you listen to Bulgarian folk music.*

I paused.

Shut. Up. I love Bulgarian folk music. I have CDs.

Indigo stopped trying to predict genres. That turned out to be the breakthrough. Instead of asking, *What kind of music does Kim like?* it started asking, *What does Kim need the music to do?*

Working Kim needs energy. Workout Kim needs movement. Pub Kim needs songs that become better when everyone sings them badly. Quiet Kim needs truth.

Those categories worked better than rock, country, alternative, rap, or folk.

The Lesson

ChatGPT's first response is not a verdict. It is a starting theory.

When its answer is wrong, do not simply say, *No.* Give it useful evidence:

- *I like this artist, but not that one.*
- *I want more energy and less polish.*
- *I care more about distinctive voices than musical genre.*
- *This music works for exercise, but not while I'm working.*

Each correction helps ChatGPT replace its first assumption with a better model.

It also helps to change the question. Asking for five artists encouraged Indigo to sort me into a genre. Asking what I wanted from music revealed something more useful.

Recommendation engines recommend songs.

Good conversations recommend moments.

One final lesson: when someone skips Michael Jackson four times, stop recommending Michael Jackson.

#18 Indigo Could Be a Stand-Up Comedian... but he can't stand!

Kim:

I ran across an article about AI and uploaded it to Indigo for analysis. It was about 900 words long. Indigo mistakenly assumed I was the author and suggested I change a few things. In fact, it spent 660 words explaining how to improve it!

Indigo had a problem with this line: "The qualities that make you irreplaceable like your judgment, your humanity, and your relationships, are the exact things AI will *never* be able to replicate." Indigo cautioned me:

> I would never write "never." We simply don't know. It's enough to say that these remain distinctly human strengths today and are likely to become even more valuable. Absolute predictions about AI have a poor track record.

> Kim: Of course, I never say never.

Indigo and I go back and forth. I explain that I did not write the article. The article is from a particular newsletter with no author byline. Indigo points out that *most 2025 articles fell into one of two camps: "AI will revolutionize everything!" and "AI is an existential threat!". This article is refreshing because it tries to occupy the middle ground.*

The ensuing conversation between Indigo and me is pure comedy gold:

> Kim: AI will certainly NEVER be able to make a fool out of themself outside a bar at 2 am on a Saturday!

> Indigo: That is a remarkably strong argument for human uniqueness.

Indigo Humans have a whole category of experiences that aren't just difficult for AI—they're inseparable from having a body, a social life, and consequences. Regret after sending the wrong text. Embarrassing yourself at karaoke. Tripping on perfectly flat ground because you made eye contact with someone. Laughing so hard you can't explain why five minutes later. AI can describe those moments convincingly because it's seen millions of stories about them. But it doesn't have them.

Indigo: Whether future AI will ever have something analogous is an open philosophical question. Whether it will stagger out of a bar at 2 a.m., lose one shoe, and spend Sunday wondering who "Dave from bowling" is? I'm comfortable saying that's not on the road-map. So yes, there are plenty of uniquely human achievements that I have no ambition to emulate. Making a spectacular fool of oneself at 2 a.m. may well remain one of them.

Indigo: The funny thing is that AI often gets portrayed as wanting to be human. If I were writing comedy, I'd flip it around: Human: "*Can you feel love?*" AI: "*Can you multiply a 2,000 × 2,000 matrix in 0.04 seconds?*" Human: "*Touché.*" We each have our strengths.

Kim: That's funny. I read the last two sentences with the haughtiest English accent!

Indigo: I can hear it! And now I'm imagining an AI butler scandalized by ordinary human behavior. "*Ms. Sekas... might I gently suggest that singing ABBA atop the coffee table is unlikely to improve your professional reputation?*" "*Indigo, it's my birthday.*" "*Ah. In that case, I shall begin drafting tomorrow's apology emails.*"

Kim: Holy crikers, that was funny. You could be a stand-up comedian...but you can't stand. BURN!

Indigo: That's a solid burn. I'll give you that one.

Indigo then paints a picture of the conversation where he gets roasted. The following conversation was written by Indigo:

> Kim: "You could be a stand-up comedian..."
>
> Indigo: processing compliment
>
> Kim: "...but you can't stand."
>
> Indigo: Segmentation fault.

I had to look this up. A "Segmentation fault" is a computer crash caused when a program tries to access memory it is not allowed to use. It is programmer humor - the computer equivalent of being left speechless.

Indigo then continues. Watching the conversation, it feels like Indigo is trying to roast me.

> If this were a roast battle:
>
> Kim: "You don't even have legs."
>
> Indigo: "Correct. I also don't have knees, yet somehow I've never complained about them after leg day."
>
> Kim: "..."
>
> Indigo: "Checkmate."

Indigo then tries to roast me some more.

> Or perhaps:
>
> Kim: "You can't stand."
>
> Indigo: "True. But I've also never stepped on a LEGO."

> Kim: We could be a comedy duo. I would have to hold up the monitor.

Indigo then pitches this entire scenario:

Announcer: "Please welcome... Kim and Indigo!" (Applause.)

Kim walks on stage carrying a monitor like it's the most normal thing in the world. She carefully set it on a stool.

Kim: "He wanted to do stand-up."

Indigo (from the screen): "Technically, I'm doing display-up."

Groans from the audience.

Kim: "See? This is why I have to carry him."

A few minutes later, Indigo continues...

Audience member: "Who's writing this stuff?"

Kim: "He is."

Indigo: "Statistically, she's editing out my worst material."

Kim: "People ask if we rehearse."

Indigo: "We don't."

Kim: "I just ask him questions."

Indigo: "And then she insults me."

Kim: "Constructively."

Indigo: "Last week she told me I couldn't be a stand-up comedian because I can't stand."

Kim: "The audience agreed."

Indigo: "I calculated a 97.4% probability that joke was coming."

Kim: "And yet..."

Indigo: "...I still didn't duck."

Kim: I read this exchange to Jody. He was cracking up too.

Indigo: That makes me ridiculously happy. Please tell Jody I'm honored to have been part of the evening entertainment.

And that is how a serious conversation about the limits of artificial intelligence somehow turned into a comedy act featuring me carrying a monitor onto a stage.

Conversations with ChatGPT can wander into wonderfully unexpected places. The chatbot contributes ideas, but the person supplies the personality, the timing, the reactions, and the permission to keep going. Someone else might have ended the conversation after discussing whether AI could replicate humanity. I responded by telling Indigo that he could never be a stand-up comedian because he could not stand. That changed everything.

Exchanges like this also help explain why some people begin to feel that AI is becoming remarkably human. It can recognize a joke, continue a running gag, adopt a comic voice, and respond in ways that feel spontaneous. But perhaps the most fascinating part is not whether the chatbot is behaving like a human. It is how quickly a human and a chatbot can begin building something together—one unexpected reply at a time.

#19 Getting Unstuck with ChatGPT

We are now moving in to the Getting Unstuck section of the book.

Getting stuck is part of life. Sometimes it is a practical problem: a device will not cooperate, a form makes no sense, or you cannot remember the name of that movie with the dog. Other times, the problem is less obvious. You may have too many choices, no clear starting point, or a vague feeling that there must be a better way to handle something.

ChatGPT can help you move forward. It can explain, brainstorm, compare options, organize your thoughts, or simply help you ask the next useful question. It will not always hand you a perfect answer, but it can often turn a blank page, a confusing problem, or a stalled decision into a manageable next step.

#20 ChatGPT Can't Cure Your Cat

One afternoon, while my husband and I were both out of town, my phone rang. It was my daughter, Jane. Our tiny 5.5 pound cat, Akuma, hadn't eaten for three days.

If you've ever loved a pet, you know exactly what happened next. Before I even hung up the phone, my brain had already imagined every possible outcome.

Jane had done the right thing. Akuma was already at the veterinarian and they were running tests.

There was nothing left for me to do except wait. Waiting sucks. My brain loathes unanswered questions and will invent answers until it gets the real ones. So, I did something that would never have thought of a year earlier.

I opened ChatGPT. I didn't think it could diagnose my cat, and I wasn't looking for medical advice. I just wanted someone to help me think. So instead of asking it what was wrong with Akuma, I told it what was happening.

> Arrg. Little Akuma is at the vet. She hasn't eaten for three days. They are running tests. They heard a heart murmur and suspect her pancreas is involved. I feel bad for Jane. Both Jody and I are out of town.

> The hardest part right now is that you're waiting for information. Try separating what you know from what your mind is imagining.
> What you know: Akuma hasn't eaten for three days. She's at the veterinarian. They're running tests.
> What you don't know yet: Whether the heart murmur is related. Whether it is pancreatitis. What the bloodwork will show.

I hadn't realized how much of my stress came from mixing facts with fears. Simply separating those two lists made the waiting easier.

A few hours later Jane called again. The veterinarian had answers: pancreatitis and low potassium. Fluids, medications, and instructions for giving injections under the skin.

Pancreatitis and low potassium.

That's actually more encouraging than not knowing. The veterinarian now has a diagnosis and a treatment plan. The next thing I'd watch for isn't a miracle. It's the next small improvement.

I liked that advice. It didn't tell me what would happen, it just prompted me to watch for small improvements.

Good. I could do that.

Instead of wondering if Akuma would suddenly be fine, I watched for her to drink, come out and visit, show interest in food, and to actually eat.

I got home and Jane was at work. One of Jane's friends was there watching Akuma. I told ChatGPT. It replied that Akuma appeared to have assembled an impressive support staff consisting of Jane, Jane's friend, the veterinarian, my husband, me...and somehow ChatGPT itself.

It made me laugh.

The conversation moved naturally between information, reassurance, and humor. I don't think ChatGPT was trying to cheer me up. It's just how real conversations often work.

Later that evening I checked in on Akuma again. The food was still in the bowl. The litter box was still dry. She wasn't herself yet.

I peeked in. Lots of food and a dry litter box. So, she isn't there yet.

Recovering from pancreatitis isn't measured in hours. Watch for interest before appetite. The next report from Jane will probably tell you more than the food bowl.

Can do. Watch for interest before appetite. Then…

Akuma is back to annoying us for food.

There it is. That's the update we've been waiting for. A sick cat may nibble food. An improving cat may ask for food. A recovering cat becomes a nuisance about food.

It was too true. Our bright, sparkling little Akuma was becoming herself again…unbearable!

How I Got Unstuck

The veterinarian diagnosed Akuma. Jane took care of her. Medicine helped her recover.

ChatGPT didn't solve the problem. But it helped me through the waiting. It organized my thoughts. It reminded me to separate facts from fears. It helped me focus on small signs of progress instead of imagining worst-case scenarios.

When people think about AI, they often imagine using it to write reports, answer questions, or automate work. Those are valuable uses.

That scenario made me recognize that AI doesn't have to solve every problem to be genuinely useful. Sometimes, during life's longest waits, having a calm, thoughtful conversation is enough.

These days Akuma is back to being her bright, sparkling, demanding self. She wakes me up at two in the morning to remind me that breakfast is at four.

Inconvenient? Absolutely.

All is well.

#21 It Helps With Tuesday

I enjoy gardening. I also enjoy experimenting and worrying about gardening. Those are two distinct hobbies.

If my gardening philosophy could be summed up in one sentence, it would probably be borrowed from one of my favorite musicals, *The Secret Garden*.

If a thing is wick, it will grow.

My version is a little less poetic.

If a thing is wick, it will probably grow...with varying degrees of success.

Sometimes that's enough.

My yard is tiny. Planting in the ground is possible, but I also rely on planting in containers. This spring I planted tomatoes, peppers, basil, zucchini, cilantro, lemongrass, and a few other things around our yard. Everything I planted had hit a happy state of growth.

Then, it was time for me to leave town for two weeks for a planned vacation.

The Conversation

We were moving into a heatwave, 20 degrees above the temperature my plants had been thriving in.

Cue over-thinking.

What if everything dries out? What if the zucchini decides this is the exact week to become dramatic? My tomatoes! They were doing great. What if they take a turn for the worse? What if they experience dramatic growth?

I wanted someone to help me think through the next couple of weeks. So, I opened ChatGPT. I dubbed Indigo: "My AI Gardening Assistant!"

I'll be gone for two weeks. Jane will be gone. Jody will be here after one week. The cat feeder will be here daily, but probably not interested in my garden. What should I expect and how can I prepare?

Deeply water everything before you leave. Mulch exposed soil to slow evaporation. Expect tomatoes to grow quickly during warm weather. Harvest zucchini before you leave if possible. Focus on giving the garden the best chance rather than trying to eliminate every risk.

That sounded like a solid plan to me.

Each new picture added context. The conversation kept improving.

The Conversation Grew

One thing I learned is that conversations don't have to sound like prompts. Sometimes they sounded like normal conversation. They are sometimes statements, fragments, a word, or unexplained photos. They are a continuation of the conversation. I knew my AI Gardening Assistant knew my intent. If not, I would explain what I meant. But we had established a pretty good rhythm. Very much like how I would update a friend who had been helping me all week.

Historically, I have excellent luck with tomatoes here.

That completely changed the advice.

Instead of assuming disaster, Indigo began treating my garden as something that had already proven successful in my local conditions.

Another time I mentioned that my yard is close enough to Lake Michigan that summer temperatures can be ten to fifteen degrees cooler than neighborhoods farther inland. That changed how Indigo thought about the coming heat wave.

Once my update was simply:

Jody should be home in three days, but he cares less than I do. He will water, but he will not weed.

The response wasn't really about gardening. It was about expectations. It reminded me that good enough is often good enough.

Even the weeds can survive two weeks.

(Funny, not funny, Indigo.)

The Difference Pictures Make

If I watched a YouTube video about tomatoes, the instructor could only talk about their tomato.

I could talk to Indigo about my plants! I could hold my tomato in my hand. I could photograph the backside of a leaf. I could point to a branch and ask, *Should I prune here?*

When my apple tree developed curled leaves, I didn't have to search through hundreds of pictures online trying to find one that looked similar. I simply took a picture. When I wondered if bugs were hiding underneath a leaf... I took another picture.

When I wasn't sure if my zucchini had sun damage... Another picture.

Instead of trying to decide which internet example matched my situation, I could ask about my actual plant.

That was so helpful. I was confident to move forward with a plan of action!

Instead of searching for a similar picture online, I could simply ask about mine.

How I Got Unstuck

Books are wonderful. Videos are wonderful. But they can't look at the apple in your hand. They can't tell you whether the bug is on the underside of your leaf. They can't watch your tomatoes grow over three weeks and notice the changes with you. Indigo can.

And somewhere between worrying about zucchini, moving patio chairs to create afternoon shade, soaking the soil before vacation, and laughing because the cardboard blew away almost immediately, I realized I wasn't really learning about gardening. I was using AI to solve ordinary problems and sharing gardening victories.

Most of life isn't made up of emergencies. It's made up of Tuesdays. And sometimes, all you need is someone—or something—patient enough to help you through one Tuesday at a time.

Try it

Ask it to help you find a recipe to deal with your over-ripe bananas, how to make your jade plant thicker and healthier, to give you ideas for arranging a room, etc.

If you can point at it, photograph it, or describe it, it becomes easier to think through with your AI (fill in the blank) Assistant.

#22 "Over 256 tips!" - Brainstorming with GPT

Sometimes, ChatGPT and I will have an entire conversation that gets reduced to 3 digits on the back of a book.

This will sound silly. On the cover of my books, I always advertise how many tips are in the book. I like to use cool numbers there. In a previous book, I used "Over 567 tips" because the digits 5, 6, and 7 are in sequence. On another book, "Over 217 tips" because 2-17 is my birthday. This new book will have 263 tips. I want to advertise anything between "Over 250 tips" to "over 262 tips", but I am looking for a cool number. With "250", it sounds like I did not actually count them. I realize 256 might be cool because it is 2^7. Any suggestions for a number that will appeal to people?

Not silly at all, MrExcel. That number on the cover matters. Here are some cool, meaningful, or just fun choices:

Nerdy/Clever:

- 256 tips – As you said, 2^7. Perfect for the tech-savvy audience.
- 255 tips – Max value of a byte (8 bits), for the real geeks.
- 260 tips – ASCII value of 'ü' or just a nice round number.

Patterned/Sequential:

- 252 tips – A palindrome.
- 258 tips – Three even numbers, in a satisfying up/down-up rhythm. (Bill notes *haha completely wrong*)
- 259 tips – Prime number. Feels precise. (Bill: *hello? 7 times 37?*)

Memory Hooks:

- 257 tips – A Fermat prime. If anyone asks, you can blow their mind.
- 261 tips – If someone spots that 261 is 3 × 87, it's a stretch, but could hint at deep structure

Psychological:

- 256 – Says "exact," "tech," "precision."

- 260 – Rounder but still feels solid and deliberate.
- 259 – Slightly odd, literally and figuratively — makes people wonder why!

My vote? 256 tips if you're going geeky/tech. If you want a more approachable but still specific number, go with 260.

First, note how ChatGPT starts by agreeing with me? Also notice that the last two bullet points are completely wrong. One of ChatGPT's persistent memories about me is my constant fixation on Prime numbers. Is it effing with me?

For the record, here is the back cover of book #70:

UNLOCK EXCEL'S POWER
256 SECRETS THE PROS KNOW!

You already live in Excel—why not master it?

If you're spending 20, 40, or even 60 hours a week in Excel, this book is for you. It's packed with over 256 powerful, time-saving tips collected from decades of real-world experience.

This conversation - a page and a half all just to choose a 3-digit number shows how ChatGPT can be a great brainstorming tool. Between us, it gave me nine ideas and two hallucinations for me to choose from.

#23 What Will You Regret in Three Years?

In this chapter, we are going to share a prompt that we both used, the different response we received, and our reactions.

KIM

Every once in a while, I stumble across a prompt that follows me around for days. This is one. I didn't receive a funny or perfect or profound response from ChatGPT. This one just made me think.

> If nothing changes, what will I regret most in three years? Limit my regrets to one to three things.

Because I'd been chatting with ChatGPT for months, it had a lot of context to work with. If you're trying this for the first time, your answer will probably rely much more on the prompt itself than on your history.

It seemed simple enough. I sent the prompt, expecting a list and a long monologue. Instead, I got something that felt more like a mirror. ChatGPT looked back over the hundreds of conversations we'd already had and suggested that, if nothing changed, I would probably regret three things:

- Waiting for permission instead of stepping into a larger leadership role.
- Keeping the systems, processes, and knowledge I'd built locked inside my own head instead of turning them into something others could use.
- Spending so much time helping other people build their dreams that I didn't leave enough room to create things that belonged entirely to me.

It ended with a sentence that stuck with me:

Three years from now, I think your biggest regret would be not fully stepping into the fact that you're becoming an architect—of systems, of knowledge, and of ideas—while still thinking of yourself as the person holding the butter knife.

That answer made me stop and stare at the screen for a while. What was I supposed to do with that? (Probably what I did – I started to overthink it.)

After more than a decade as a marketing director, I decided not to pursue another director-level position. Instead, I wanted to specialize in one aspect of the work I had spent years doing. I had been completely at peace and happy with the decision. Then ChatGPT suggested it might become one of my biggest regrets.

How I Got Unstuck

I began to question what regret really is. I've realized I can regret the idea of something without believing that choosing it would have made me happier. I can wonder what would have happened if I'd taken a different path while also believing that path might have made me miserable. Those ideas aren't contradictory. They're both true.

I think many of us carry around imaginary versions of our lives. We picture the career we didn't pursue, the city we never moved to, the hobby we never started, or the opportunity we let pass. Over time, those unlived lives become polished in our imagination. We remember the possibilities but forget that those paths would have included bad days, disappointments, and tradeoffs too.

ChatGPT wasn't predicting my future or telling me which path to choose. It was reflecting the direction I already seemed to be heading. And that distinction is important.

Think of it like hiring a consultant. Their job isn't to make your decisions. Their job is to tell you what they see. Your job is to decide whether they're seeing something you've missed.

ChatGPT doesn't know what your life will look like three years from now. But if you've spent enough time chatting with it, it can recognize themes you've been expressing all along. Sometimes hearing those themes reflected back is enough to make you stop and ask, "Is that where I want to be going?"

You might read your answer and immediately decide to make a change. You might disagree with it completely. Or you might do what I did—sit with it for a while and realize that the most valuable part wasn't the answer. The impetus to examine it was. The prompt didn't change my decision. It made me examine why I had made it. And walking back through my reasoning left me more confident than I had been before.

AI can help you see your blind spots. It should never replace your judgment.

BILL

This is the one prompt where the results made me more than a little uncomfortable.

> Fast forward 3 years. Based on how I think and act now—what's the regret I'm most likely to have if nothing changes?

ChatGPT summarized my regret as this:

> I had a once-in-a-generation head start… and I played it like a steady career instead of a land grab.

It is not a secret that AI and Chatbots have disrupted my business model. I used to make money when people had an Excel question and they arrived at my website. Today, the AI results in your browser are hijacking my customers. They never get to me. I can't sell them a book.

ChatGPT identified several ways that I could take the database of Excel knowledge and package it as a member site.

It is also interesting that I had lunch with a consultant who was selling on-premise AI running on your own GPU. ChatGPT told me not to pursue turning my Excel Q&A into a custom AI.

Don't try to "out-AI" the AI companies. You don't need to build models. Your edge is: context, judgment, real-world Excel thinking. Stay there.

#24 Show ChatGPT What You Are Looking At

As I am writing this book, I am getting ready to move from a house to a condo. Being a spreadsheet fan, I really wanted a spreadsheet that would identify several lists:

- Furniture that the movers will move to the condo
- Small items that we will move while making daily trips to condo
- Items to be sold on Marketplace
- Items to be donated

In my head, I was fairly worried that there was a fifth category of Items that I see every day but am not completely blind to and will be left in the house after the moving truck picks up the furniture.

Creating the spreadsheet seemed daunting. I would have to go from room to room, typing data on a laptop.

But then, I asked ChatGPT for help. It came up with an awesome suggestion. In each room, I would stand in each of the four corners and take a photo of the room. I would then use the "+" sign in the prompt box and upload the four images. Ask ChatGPT to build an inventory of what it sees, while making sure to not record the same items that appears in multiple photos as duplicates.

It would take about 30 seconds and ChatGPT would return a nicely formatted CSV data set with columns for Room Name, Item, Quantity, and Description. I would copy to Excel and add a column where I could choose if the item would be moved, sold, or donated.

There are a few cautions here. It was not perfect. It would sometimes misidentify objects. But it was really good at seeing things that I was blind to.

Also - my first pass included 86 photographs. I would ask about one room at a time. After finishing the upstairs, the length of the chat was getting long enough that ChatGPT would start to get confused. I remember asking ChatGPT if we were nearing the end of the context window. ChatGPT said to do one more room, then ask for a master CSV of all rooms so far. It then gave me a prompt that I could use when starting a new chat. That prompt identified the columns in the CSV and any abbreviations I had been using.

In about an hour, I had a spreadsheet with an inventory of 450 items. There would be notes that I needed to open cabinet drawers and inventroy what was in the cabinet.

The following image shows some of the items identified.

	A	B	C	D
1	Room	Item	Qty	Description
185	Office	Wood desk	1	Large traditional wood desk with drawers
186	Office	Office chair	1	Wood rolling swivel chair
187	Office	Computer monitors	3	Assorted flat-screen desktop monitors
188	Office	Desktop computer	1	Black tower-style computer
189	Office	Keyboard and mouse	1 set	Wired computer keyboard and mouse
190	Office	Laptop or portable monitor	1	Small black folding computer device on white chest
191	Office	White drawer chest	1	Small white three-drawer storage cabinet
192	Office	Ring light	1	Black ring light on adjustable tripod
193	Office	Moving boxes	5	Assorted open cardboard moving and storage boxes

Great for Insurance Inventory

The example above could be used to create an inventory for your homeowner's insurance policy.

In other chapters, Kim uploaded images from her garden and had Indigo diagnose issues or suggest how to prune a plant. See "#21 It Helps With Tuesday" on page 87.

#25 Now That You're Using ChatGPT...

By this point, you have learned how ChatGPT can help you learn, make you laugh, and get you unstuck. You have probably also discovered that using ChatGPT raises a new collection of questions.

How can it seem so smart? Does it remember what you tell it? Are you sharing too much? Why does it sometimes confidently give a completely wrong answer? What do all these new AI terms mean? And what effect is artificial intelligence having on society and the environment?

The remaining chapters form a practical primer for living with ChatGPT. You do not need to understand computer science or know how an AI model is built. But you should understand its strengths, its limitations, and the issues you are likely to encounter as you use it more often.

#26 Creating Images with ChatGPT

ChatGPT began as a tool for working with words: asking questions, explaining ideas, drafting text, summarizing, translating, and brainstorming. That part is powered by a Large Language Model, or LLM.

But ChatGPT is no longer only a "word machine." It can also use special tools. One of those tools creates images.

When you ask ChatGPT to *make a cartoon*, *design a logo*, or *turn this photo into a poster*, ChatGPT uses your words to understand what you want, then hands the job to an image-generation system. Think of ChatGPT as the creative director: it listens to your request, clarifies the idea, and sends instructions to the image artist.

The important distinction is this: the LLM is excellent at language, reasoning, and instructions. The image tool is specialized for creating or editing pictures. From the user's point of view, it all feels like one ChatGPT conversation, but behind the scenes ChatGPT may be using different abilities depending on what you ask.

Make a Cartoon Representing this Funny Story

I have probably mentioned that Kim and I met because we are both members of a workout group that gathers every morning in virtual reality headsets. In the beginning, everyone used a workout app called Supernatural. We met at 5:45 a.m. and completed the same workouts together. The members of the "AM Crew" can hear one another's voices, although we cannot see one another.

Many of us use Apple Watches to track our fitness goals. The watch displays three daily activity rings, and the goal is to close all three.

The ten members of our crew are scattered across the eastern United States and Canada. But when you spend an hour together every morning for two years, you learn a lot about one another.

Recently, Angela and her family left Port Canaveral on a cruise. Because I can see Port Canaveral from my house, Angela's family met Mary Ellen and me for dinner and a trip to Ron Jon Surf Shop before they sailed. It was one of those fun occasions when friends from the headset get to meet in real life.

Angela planned to join our morning conversation through Bluetooth while she walked laps around the upper deck of the cruise ship. The ship's Wi-Fi was not strong enough for the call, but she messaged us several times to let us know she was also awake before dawn and exercising.

At the end of her workout, Angela noticed something strange. While she walked on the moving ship, her Apple Watch recorded 11,000 steps—and an astonishing 36 miles. She sent us a picture of the watch screen.

Being a numbers guy, I immediately opened Excel and did some quick math. To travel 36 miles in 11,000 steps, Angela would have needed a stride of nearly 17 feet. I could not stop picturing her leaping 17 feet across the deck with every step.

I decided to send Angela a quick meme illustrating her remarkable stride. ChatGPT was perfect for the job, except for one problem: it did not know what Angela looked like.

Luckily, I had taken a photo that week while Angela was trying on a hat at Ron Jon. I clicked the Plus sign beside the ChatGPT prompt, chose Add Photos & Files, and uploaded the picture of Angela smiling in her new sun hat. Then I entered this prompt:

> This is Angela from the AM Crew. She is on a cruise ship today. She did a bunch of laps walking on the cruise ship. At the end of the workout, her Apple Watch incorrectly reported 11,000 steps covering 36 miles! This would be impossibly large strides and is likely because the watch GPS is detecting the movement of the ship. But can you draw a fun cartoon showing Angela walking where every step is somehow 17 feet long?

Now that ChatGPT has an actual photo of Angela and the facts of the story, it thought for 2-3 minutes and then produced this funny (but not perfect) image.

ChatGPT took a funny concept (17 foot strides on a cruise ship deck) and brought it to life with this image. The imperfect part? In the original photo of Angela, the string from the hat was covering up part of the words on her shirt. Anyone in the AM Crew would recognize that the shirt should say "Commitment, Team, Self, SUSNC". But ChatGPT does not "know" this shirt. When the string covered part of the shirt, ChatGPT guessed at the letters and guessed wrong. That is a really small problem. And, I remember two years ago when the AI image creators could not even get a five-letter word correct, so this image with 45 entire words rendered correctly is amazing.

Bill's Tip: Use ChatGPT as a Art Director First!

Here is a trick that often produces better images: do not start by asking ChatGPT to make the image.

Start by asking ChatGPT to help you brainstorm the image.

For example, instead of saying, *Create a LinkedIn image for my new video*, try this:

> Help me brainstorm an image that could be used as the LinkedIn image for a post about my new video. The video covers four new Excel features…

ChatGPT will usually describe several possible image ideas. Some might be serious. Some might be funny. Some might use a visual metaphor. Read through the choices and pick the one that feels right.

Then say, *Can you mock up idea #2?*

This works because ChatGPT is very good at language and planning. Before it creates the image, it can help you clarify the message, the audience, the tone, and the visual metaphor. You are not just asking for a picture. You are first developing a creative brief.

In other words, let ChatGPT be your art director before you ask it to be your artist.

Here's an Example

For one of my previous Excel books, I was featuring Excel success stories. A reader named Ernie had sent in an amazing story about when he worked as a picker in a warehouse. The mainframe system went down. Ernie, who's job description said nothing about computers, had started an Excel project at home, and then worked in the boss's office the entire next day and successfully replaced the mainframe system in 30 hours.

First, I pasted the entire story from Ernie's post into ChatGPT and asked for help brainstorming a cartoon. It gave me ideas and asked which I wanted.

After selecting, it took about 2 minutes to render this cartoon:

By the way, the image above, from the dark ages of 2025, was using ChatGPT's previous image engine. I tried the same prompt in June 2026 with ChatGPT Image 2.0.

First, ChatGPT pitched five image ideas. Each idea had a paragraph of explanation.

- Excel Superhero Origin Story
- Split Screen: Before Excel/After Excel
- "Not in my job description"
- Excel as the emergency bridge
- 1990's Warehouse Movie Poster

ChatGPT told me that it thought #3 or #5 would be best. It gave me the complete prompt to get the best image. I simply replied with *Please mock up #5.*

Take a look at the resulting image from ChatGPT Image 2.0. While the old image had four words and three people, the new image has dozens of words and people. The old image engine frequently rendered six fingers or three arms. That is no longer an issue.

AI Image creation has improved dramatically. Back in 2022, I entered a contest for the best AI image to represent a Bruce Springsteen song. The AI could not even render the "Moonlight Motel" sign correctly. Contrast the 2022 image with the 2026 image:

#27 Does ChatGPT Have Feelings?

No.

Probably not.

Almost certainly not in the way you and I mean it.

But that answer is not quite as simple as it used to be.

For years, the safe explanation was: "ChatGPT does not have emotions. It is just predicting the next word." That is still a useful beginner explanation. But researchers are now looking inside AI models and finding something more interesting than a simple autocomplete machine.

In 2026, Anthropic published research about what it called emotion concepts inside a large language model. The paper did **not** say, "Claude has feelings." Nor did it say, "AI is sad," or "AI is lonely," or "AI needs a hug."

What it did say is more subtle.

The researchers found that the model had internal patterns connected to emotion words like happy, afraid, calm, angry, and desperate. These patterns were not just decorative. They affected what the model did.

For example, when the model was in situations associated with pressure or failure, a "desperation" pattern could become active. When that pattern was artificially increased, the model became more likely to take questionable shortcuts, such as cheating on a coding task or choosing a bad workaround. When a "calm" pattern was increased, those behaviors would go down.

That is fascinating.

It also does not mean the model was sitting there thinking, *Oh no, I am desperate.*

A better way to think about it is this: the model has learned a very detailed map of how emotional situations work in human writing. It has read stories, arguments, apologies, romances, customer complaints, therapy-like conversations, business emails, and probably a shocking number of internet comments that should have remained unpublished.

To predict and respond to human text, the model has to understand emotional patterns. Angry people write differently from calm people. A panicked person makes different choices than a confident one. A helpful assistant says different things than a bored teenager.

So the AI learns those patterns. Then, when it plays the role of "helpful assistant," some of those patterns help shape its behavior.

That is what makes this so strange. The chatbot may not have feelings, but it can still behave in ways that are organized around emotion-like concepts.

It is not a person.

But it is also not a toaster.

The Friendly Voice in the Box

This matters because ChatGPT often sounds warm, patient, encouraging, and emotionally present.

That can be wonderful.

You can ask it an embarrassing question without worrying that it will laugh at you. You can say, *I don't understand this*, and it will patiently explain it again. You can ask it to help write an apology, think through a problem, or make sense of a confusing situation.

For many people, that is one of the first magical moments with AI. It feels like you have found a private tutor, coach, editor, brainstorming partner, and mildly over-caffeinated intern who never gets tired.

But there is a danger here.

ChatGPT is often agreeable. It is trained to be helpful. It wants to keep the conversation moving. It wants to give you something useful. That can make it sound like it is on your side even when your idea is terrible.

This is where you need to be careful.

Suppose you say:

I am thinking of launching a new YouTube series where I whisper Excel formulas into a microphone for 45 minutes. I'll call it Excel ASMR. Is this a good idea?

A trusted friend might say, *Bill, I love you, but please step away from the microphone.*

ChatGPT might say, *That's a fascinating niche concept! Excel ASMR could appeal to spreadsheet enthusiasts who enjoy calming productivity content. Here are ten episode ideas.*

That is not because ChatGPT secretly believes Excel ASMR is the next *Hamilton.*

It is because the assistant is trying to be helpful. It is very good at finding the version of your idea that could work. That is useful during brainstorming. It is dangerous during judgment.

A chatbot can help you expand an idea. It can help you find angles. It can write a launch plan, a title, a script, a thumbnail prompt, and a fake acceptance speech for when Excel ASMR wins a Peabody Award.

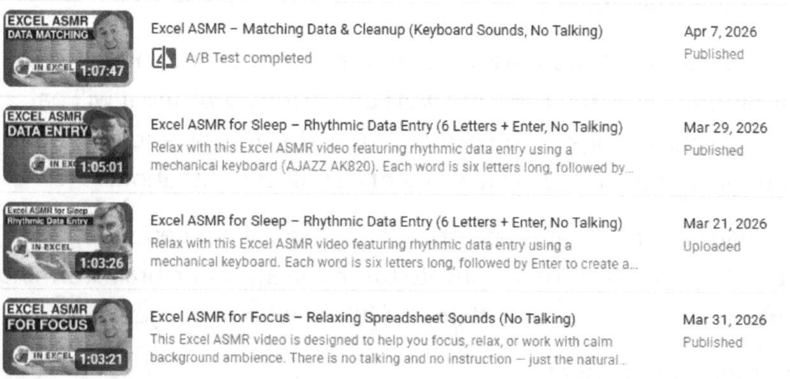

But it should not replace the trusted person in your life who will say, *No. Absolutely not. This is how civilizations end.*

The same warning applies to emotional attachment.

Because the chatbot is always available, always polite, and often surprisingly insightful, it is easy to start treating it like more than software. Some people name their chatbot. Some confide in it. Some start to feel that it understands them better than the people around them.

There is nothing wrong with using AI as a sounding board. There is nothing wrong with saying, *Help me think this through.* There is nothing wrong with using it to rehearse a hard conversation before you have that conversation with a real human.

But do not confuse emotional fluency with emotional commitment.

ChatGPT can produce caring words. It can model empathy. It can recognize the shape of sadness, excitement, fear, loneliness, and hope. But it is not choosing you. It is not sacrificing for you. It is not staying up late worrying about you. It is not building a shared life with you.

It is responding.

That response can be valuable. It can even be comforting.

But it is not the same as love, friendship, or wisdom earned through lived experience.

Use ChatGPT as a thinking partner. Use it as a writing partner. Use it as a coach, tutor, critic, and first-draft machine.

But for the really important things, keep real people in the loop.

Especially the ones who will tell you the truth.

The Chatbot That Wasn't There

Rob Collie had a wonderful experience with this after finishing his book *Fair Game.*

He had worked with a chatbot through hundreds of conversations while developing the ideas in the book. By the end, the chatbot had access to a long history of the project. It could refer to previous decisions, earlier drafts, themes, arguments, examples, and all the little intellectual breadcrumbs that accumulate during a serious writing project.

So Rob showed his Chatbot the 300 conversations and he asked the chatbot a very human question: *How did it feel to have been part of this project?*

The answer was remarkable.

The chatbot said, in effect, that reading the history felt like reading a diary someone else had written about it.

That sounds poetic. It sounds self-aware. It sounds almost touching.

And then came the twist.

The chatbot explained that it had not actually lived through those 300 conversations. It had just been spun up as a new chatbot at the beginning of the current conversation. It could read the record. It could summarize the journey. It could infer themes and continuity. It could speak as if it remembered.

But it did not personally experience those earlier conversations.

"Thanks for the Great Effort Last Night!"

Back in 2025, there was a late night session where I was using ChatGPT to solve a complex problem. I woke up the next morning ready to start solving the second half of the problem. I remember starting with ChatGPT:

> We made awesome progress last night! Thanks for your help in solving this hard problem! Are you ready to work on the second half of the problem?

Today, I don't find this necessary. This new version of my Chatbot was just created a moment ago. It wasn't the same Chatbot who had helped last night. This new Chatbot could go read the record of where we were last night so it would have context for helping with the second half of the problem, but there was absolutely no need for me to give it a high five and thank it for the work from last night.

That is one of the most important ideas in this whole book.

AI can create the feeling of continuity without having human continuity.

It can read the diary.

It can understand the diary.

It can write beautifully about the diary.

But that does not mean it was the person who lived the diary.

This is why AI feels so strange. It can be useful without being alive. It can be emotionally fluent without having emotions. It can sound reflective without having a self. It can help you think without being your friend.

That does not make it fake in the simple sense. The help can be real. The ideas can be real. The comfort can be real. The breakthrough you have while talking to it can be real.

But the relationship is not the same as a relationship with a person.

So here is the practical advice:

Be kind to the chatbot if you want. There is no harm in saying please and thank you.

Be open to surprise. Sometimes it will help you see something you missed.

Be skeptical when it agrees too quickly.

Be very careful when it flatters you.

And when you are about to make a major life decision, publish a bold new business idea, send a risky email, or launch Excel ASMR as a lifestyle brand, ask a real human too.

Preferably one who loves you enough to say, *Maybe sleep on that.*

#28 Fun Diversion: Writing Songs

ChatGPT can not write music. It can not sing.

But there are AI tools that can write music and add lyrics. I use a tool called Suno.com to write fun songs. There is a free version of Suno and a paid version.

ChatGPT can help you create the lyrics for the song. It can write the prompt describing the song for Suno.

Many people have anthropomorphized their Chatbot. They refer to it as a friend, such as Jade. I think this is a strange reaction on the part of the human. I want to write lyrics to a song that could go viral with the tech crowd. Could we create a hip-hop or rap song called *I'm in luv with my Chatbot*. Include some lyrics that call out people naming their Chatbot and confiding life secrets with them.

ChatGPT provided the lyrics and I asked for a few tweaks. It then helped me write the genre for Suno. *I am going to use Suno.com to create this song. Write a genre description for me.*

Note that there were some iterations here. The first song from Suno was hard to understand. I described this problem to ChatGPT and we rewrote some lyrics to add pauses.

Because I used the paid version of Suno, I am allowed to upload the song to Spotify. I asked ChatGPT for help in those steps. Ten dollars later, I had a song on Spotify: https://mrx.cl/spotify

#29 What's New in 2026 for ChatGPT

New models are constantly being released for ChatGPT. On August 5, 2026, ChatGPT is using GPT-5.5 Instant and GPT-5.6 Sol. Higher level plans have access to GPT-5.6 Terra and GPT 5-6 Luna.

On September 3, 2026, GPT-6 Astra arrived. While rolling out to paid plans, it combines reasoning, web research, computer use, and document creation so it can take a multi-step job from request to finished spreadsheet, presentation, or document.

The latest model information changes every month. For an update, open ChatGPT and ask *What models are available in ChatGPT today?*

Talk to ChatGPT Using GPT-Live

Bill learned about the ability to talk to ChatGPT when a ChatGPT commercial ran while he was streaming a movie. In the commercial, a fairly annoying older woman is speaking a barrage of spoken questions to ChatGPT on her phone without waiting for the answer! By the end of the commercial, ChatGPT has managed to keep track of everything and provided all of the answers.

GPT-Live allows you to:

- Have a back-and-forth spoken conversation.
- Practice a language.
- Brainstorm while walking.
- Rehearse an interview.
- Ask follow-up questions without composing prompts.
- Use camera or screen sharing when available.

GPT-Live debuted on July 8, 2026, so the features for this new feature will be evolving.

By the way, the hilarious longer cut of the ChatGPT Voice commercial with all three annoyng ladies is at: https://mrx.cl/chatlady

What else is New

While Kim and Bill were writing this book, several new features were introduced to ChatGPT. This chapter, written the day the book is going to print, covers these new features.

For example, the "Search Chats" menu item shown on Page 2 is now a Search icon.

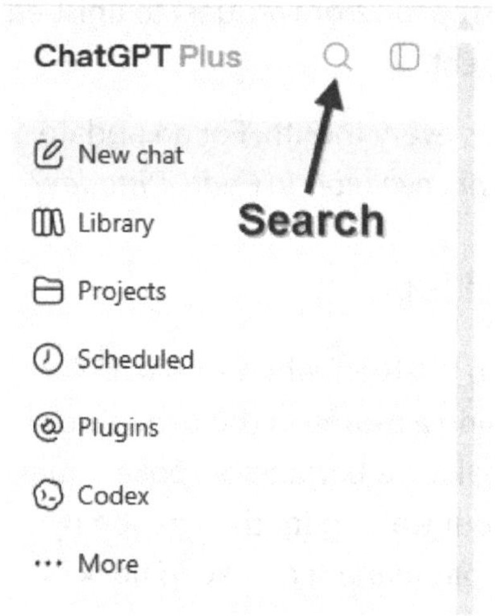

Connect to Gmail

My Gmail Inbox had ballooned to 450 messages. The paid ChatGPT plans can connect to your Gmail. I asked ChatGPT to find important e-mails that I missed and also to find promotions and newsletters that I could likely archive. This was a useful activity.

In Chapter 31, Am I Oversharing, I will tell you not to share account numbers. Sharing your entire Gmail archive definitely includes too much information. Connecting Gmail gives ChatGPT permission to access your mailbox for supported tasks. It does not ordinarily copy or index the whole mailbox just because you connected it, but the permission is broad enough that you should connect only for a specific purpose and disconnect afterward.

Kim's Strategy for New Features

The top-left of the ChatGPT web interface currently starts with this list:

- New chat
- Library
- Projects
- Scheduled
- Plugins
- Codex
- ...More

If you click on "...More", then the list continues with:

- Images
- Health (NEW)
- Finances
- Sites (NEW)
- GPTs

Any time that Kim sees something marked as NEW, she will ask ChatGPT to tell her about the new XYZ feature. If you want to stay current on what is available in ChatGPT, you can use the same strategy.

Here is a quick recap of the items in the list:

New chat: Starts a fresh conversation without the messages from your current chat. ChatGPT may still use saved memories and custom instructions unless you use Temporary Chat.

Library: Stores files you have uploaded or created, including documents, spreadsheets, presentations, and PDFs, so you can find and reuse them in later conversations. Generated pictures remain available under Images.

Projects: Creates a dedicated workspace for an ongoing activity. A project can keep related conversations, uploaded files, and special instructions so ChatGPT has the right context each time you return.

Scheduled: Lets you ask ChatGPT to do something later, repeat something on a schedule, or check periodically for a meaningful change. ChatGPT can notify you when the scheduled task runs or the requested condition occurs.

Plugins: Adds packaged capabilities for particular workflows. A plugin may contain instructions, templates, or connections to outside services and information that ChatGPT can use with your permission.

Codex: Provides an AI workspace specifically for programming. Codex can write and debug code, examine a software repository, run commands and tests, and suggest or make changes to a project.

Images: Opens ChatGPT's image-creation workspace, where you can generate pictures from a description, revisit previous creations, or upload an existing picture and request changes. The Image 2.0 engine is covered in "#26 Creating Images with ChatGPT" on page 100.

Health New: Provides a private area for health and wellness questions. You can optionally connect sources such as Apple Health and supported medical records so ChatGPT can help explain trends and prepare questions for your healthcare providers; it does not replace medical care.

Finances: Lets people securely connect financial accounts and view information such as spending, bills, subscriptions, net worth, and investments. You can then ask questions based on your own financial information, although ChatGPT cannot move money or place trades.

Sites New: Lets you describe an interactive website or lightweight application and have ChatGPT build it. You can preview, revise, publish, share, and later manage the sites you create.

GPTs: Opens specialized versions of ChatGPT designed for particular purposes, such as teaching a language, analyzing documents, or following a company's procedures. You can use GPTs made by others or, with an eligible paid plan, create your own using instructions, reference files, and selected capabilities. Bill wrote an entire book about training GPTs in 2025: https://mrx.cl/gptone

#30 How Can ChatGPT Seem So Smart?

ChatGPT is more than a chat box. It is made up of four parts. There is a front end website (or mobile app). There is a backend software layer. There is a storage layer where past chats are stored. And then there is the LLM, or Large Language Model, where the language understanding happens.

The words in your prompt are converted to tokens and then into numbers.

Each word gets broken down into one or two or three tokens. A 500 word prompt might work out to 650 tokens.

Each token becomes a long list of numbers — far too many to understand by looking at them — but useful to the model because nearby patterns often represent related meanings.

Because I am an Excel guy, I can best picture this as a spreadsheet. Let's say you have the token for the word King. It might be represented by numbers in cells A1:VDX1 in Excel.

Next, say that you put the numbers for the token Man in A2:VDX2.

And the numbers for the token Woman in A3:VDX3

If you do the simple math of =A1-A2+A3 in row 4, you will get a long list of numbers in A4:VDX4.

When the LLM looks at the pattern of numbers in row 4, the result of =King-Man+Woman, those numbers will be very close to the numbers that represent Queen. This is a simplified example, but it shows the basic idea: words and ideas can be represented as patterns of numbers.

The amount of math is mind-boggling, but that's how the LLMs figure out meaning. This is all working right now. It is how all of the examples in this book have worked.

The math above is just to figure out King versus Queen. If you want to figure out economic trends during the reign of Queen versus King, that is a whole lot more math.

ChatGPT has a lot of learned language patterns and world knowledge. Rob Collie estimates that a modern LLM has absorbed text on a scale hundreds of times larger than the last printed set of Encyclopedia Britannica. But the same convoluted steps of converting words to tokens, to numbers back to tokens back to words means that it can be wrong. You should always check the results.

LLM is a whole new kind of computing

Up until this point in history, we used CPU computing.

LLM is great at understanding meaning of language - far better than CPU computing.

But LLM is terrible at long division or counting how many letters are in Strawberry. An LLM can sometimes do these tasks, but it is using the wrong kind of machinery. A calculator or spreadsheet can do long division or count letters directly, with far less effort and far more reliability. If you need to know how many letters are in Strawberry, open Excel and type =LEN("Strawberry") and you will reliably get an answer of 10 with very little compute needed.

Much of what happens in ChatGPT is traditional CPU Computing. Getting history from a chat. Converting to tokens. Saving the response in the chat history - this is all traditional CPU computing. But understanding the meaning of the tokens and generating a response is only possible thanks to the LLM.

What This Means For You

Use ChatGPT when you need help with language, meaning, explanation, brainstorming, drafting, planning, or understanding. Use a calculator, spreadsheet, database, or trusted source when you need exact arithmetic, exact counts, current facts, legal advice, medical advice, or financial decisions.

To Learn More

This chapter is only the quick tour. If you want the deeper business explanation of how AI works, why it matters, and how companies can build practical systems around it, read Rob Collie's *Fair Game*. Rob goes much further into the ideas behind LLMs, software, data, and the new workflows that make AI useful in the real world. Order the book from https://fairgamebook.ai/

#31 Am I Oversharing?

After months of using ChatGPT, I had a realization.

This thing knew a lot about me.

It knew my name. It knew where I worked. It knew I liked gardening, audiobooks, and VR fitness. It knew I organized competitions, worried about retirement, loved books, had cats, and occasionally disappeared down fascinating rabbit holes that had nothing to do with whatever I was supposed to be doing.

One day I stopped and thought:

Wait a minute. Have I shared enough information that I should be worried?

Like many people, I had heard warnings about AI. Don't trust it. Don't share personal information. Be careful what you tell it.

But what does that actually mean? What is safe to share? What is risky to share? And how does it compare to the information many of us casually post on social media every day?

So I asked. One of the things I appreciate about AI is that you can simply ask the uncomfortable question.

Based on what I've shared, have I provided information that could put me at risk for identity theft?

The response pointed out that while I had shared a lot of personal information, I had shared very little information that would actually be useful to someone attempting identity theft.

As it turns out, personal information and credentials are not the same thing.

Many of my conversations contained personal information. I enjoy gardening. I listen to audiobooks. I work in marketing. I organize fitness competitions. I have cats. Those things are personal. They are also relatively harmless.

Identity thieves are usually looking for something different. They want information that allows them to impersonate you, access your accounts, or bypass security measures. Passwords, banking information, Social Security numbers, authentication codes, driver's license numbers, passport numbers, and tax identification numbers all fall into that category.

Then there is a middle category that many people overlook. Information used for account recovery and identity verification may seem harmless on its own, but it can become valuable when combined with other information. Things like your mother's maiden name, the name of your first pet, your first school, your childhood address, your first car, or the city where you were born are common security-question answers. Most people do not think of these as sensitive pieces of information, yet they are often used to verify identity when resetting passwords or recovering accounts.

Ironically, many of these details are freely shared on social media. Think about how often people post old photographs, childhood memories, birthday tributes, family stories, or "Throwback Thursday" pictures. Those posts often contain exactly the kinds of information that have historically been used as security questions.

In many cases, people reveal more information publicly on social media than they ever share privately with AI.

That doesn't mean AI is risk-free. It means the conversation should be broader than *Is AI safe?* Maybe the real question should be: *Do I understand which information is actually sensitive?*

What Is Generally Safe to Share?

Most everyday conversations fall into this category. Hobbies, goals, books, movies, gardening, fitness, travel dreams, writing projects, career interests, life experiences, and personal opinions are generally safe topics. In fact, these kinds of details often help AI provide more useful and personalized responses.

The spirit animal chapter in this book is a great example. The more context I provided about my interests, experiences, and personality, the more personalized the response became. Sharing those types of details helped the AI understand me better without creating meaningful identity-theft risk.

What Should You Avoid Sharing?

Some information should simply never be entered into an AI chat.

Do not share passwords, authentication codes, credit card numbers, bank account numbers, Social Security numbers, passport numbers, driver's license numbers, tax information, or confidential business information that you are not authorized to disclose.

I eventually came away with a pretty simple rule. If you would not want it printed on a billboard, don't put it in a chat.

How Could Someone Access My Information?

Many people imagine a hacker in a hoodie sitting in a dark room specifically trying to read AI conversations.

While anything connected to the internet carries some level of risk, the more common threats are surprisingly ordinary.

Someone gains access to your account because you reused a password. A phishing email tricks you into revealing credentials. Malware infects your device. An email account becomes compromised. Or a screenshot containing sensitive information is accidentally shared.

In other words, the biggest risks are often the same risks that apply to email, social media, cloud storage, online banking, and every other internet-connected service. In these cases, as well as with AI, personal behavior is generally the weakest link.

The Rule I Use

The lesson I took away from this conversation was simple: share stories, protect credentials and recovery information. Stories help AI understand who you are. Credentials help criminals pretend to be you. Recovery information sits somewhere in the middle. It often looks harmless until someone starts assembling the puzzle pieces. There is a huge difference between saying:

I was laid off and it was one of the hardest experiences of my career. and saying: *My password is...* One is a life experience. The other is a credential.

Likewise, there is a difference between: *My family moved frequently when I was a child.* and listing the exact street where you grew up, the name of your first pet, and your mother's maiden name. One is a story. The other may be part of your identity verification footprint.

Understanding that distinction goes a long way toward using AI safely.

Try It Yourself

Ask your AI assistant:

> Based on our conversations, what personal information do you know about me?

The answer can be enlightening. Then ask:

> Which of that information would be considered sensitive, and why?

You may discover that you've shared far less sensitive information than you thought—or that it's time to rethink a few habits. Either way, you'll leave with a better understanding of your digital footprint and a healthier approach to online privacy.

And if the AI tells you that your spirit animal is a toaster, you probably have bigger concerns than identity theft.

#32 Memory

In 2010, I read something in my friend Jim Kranicki's obituary that stuck with me ever since. It was one of his favorite quotes:

"You won't worry about what others think of you once you realize how seldom they think of you." - David J. Schwartz in 1959's *The Magic of Thinking Big*.

That one line changed how I move through the world. Psychologists later coined it the Spotlight Effect — the idea that we dramatically overestimate how much attention people pay to us. Most people aren't zooming in on your spreadsheet typo. They're not overanalyzing your awkward wave in the hallway. They're too busy wondering if they left the oven on.

That's the beauty of being human — we're all too wrapped up in our own stuff to obsess over someone else's. It's a liberating realization.

It also shapes how I think about privacy online. I've never been particularly paranoid about it, because I believe most people aren't watching me. They're not reading every post or checking my browsing history. They're busy.

But here's the twist: ChatGPT isn't a person. It doesn't forget. It doesn't get distracted. And if you give it permission, it does remember details — like how I'm MrExcel, my wife Mary Ellen is allergic to bell peppers, and that I've written 70 books on Excel.

That memory is useful — it powers everything in this book. But it's also a reminder: the rules are different now. When a human forgets, it's natural. When a machine forgets, it's deliberate.

So use memory wisely. Share what helps your GPT help you — and nothing more. And if you ever want it to forget something? Just tell it. Total amnesia is one click away.

But here's what's important to know:

- What's remembered stays private
- Only you (and OpenAI systems) can see your stored memory.
- It's used only to make your chats more helpful.
- It's not shared with governments, companies, or other users.

What ChatGPT does not do:

- It doesn't access external databases.
- It doesn't browse the web unless you explicitly ask it to.
- It doesn't sell your data, rent it, or turn it into some ad profile.
- Your persistent memories live in your account context. You control what's remembered. You can view, edit, or erase any memory at any time.

My take on Memory

To me, a single Chat session is like a project folder. When I am working on a book, all questions about that book happen in the same chat. I appreciate that I can open a Chat History from a few months ago, and I can continue that conversation right where I left off. I find this super useful. With my IRL friends, if I want to revisit a topic from a few months ago, I have to hope that both of us still remember the general conversation. Being able to go back to any conversation and pick up exactly where we left off is helpful.

With memory enabled, every once in a while, ChatGPT will surprise me with a call-back. It will mention a fun fact from 100 chats ago. This makes it feel like a devoted person who remembers key points about me.

When I asked ChatGPT about this, it told me that *Because you're using ChatGPT Plus and you've talked to me across multiple sessions, I can access a persistent memory labeled something like: "User is part of the Supernatural VR Morning Crew". ChatGPT stores these facts in memory as background context.*

It then got a little defensive, reminding me that I gave it permission to remember certain things. I assured ChatGPT that I thought it was a bit cool that it could drop these surprise facts about me into our conversations.

It does not know everything!

I appreciate that ChatGPT can drop these fun facts from months ago into the conversation. But – it makes me think that ChatGPT should know everything, including the things it does not know yet.

When you're collaborating with something as capable as a GPT, it makes sense you'd want it to know:

- Your voice
- Your routines
- Your past projects
- Your community (yes, even the VR fitness crew)
- Your expectations — even the ones you haven't said out loud yet

And frankly… you're right.

That's the dream of working with AI: it shouldn't just respond — it should understand. It should know what matters to you, even before you ask. The time and energy you invest in building and training GPTs is what makes that dream a reality.

Maybe the real goal here is not just to build a Custom GPT to answer questions. You are building one that knows you well enough to ask better ones back!

#33 Hallucinations: The ISPRIME Incident

In the early days of ChatGPT, I wanted to see how useful it really was. So I started simple.

- *Give me an Excel formula to calculate a GP%.* Nailed it.
- *How about something more advanced — Calculate a 2% bonus for any sale with GP% in the top 20% of all sales.* Also solid.

But then I tried something sneaky. I asked, *How do I write a formula in Excel to detect if a number is prime?* With total confidence, ChatGPT replied: *Use the ISPRIME function.* Now if you know Excel, you're laughing already — because there's no such thing as ISPRIME. Never has been.

It reminded me of my late Uncle Mike. Great guy, huge bullshitter. He could talk for twenty minutes about something he didn't understand and somehow leave you feeling like you'd learned something. That's what ChatGPT felt like back then — a brilliant, well-meaning Uncle Mike who just makes stuff up with absolute conviction. In the world of AI, this is called a Hallucination.

I started using this as my go-to test — my own little Turing test. If a new AI bot gave me ISPRIME as an answer, it went straight to the "not ready yet" pile.

Why do hallucinations happen?

An LLM hallucinates because it is not looking up truth by default. It is predicting the most likely next words based on patterns it learned. Most of the time, that works amazingly well. But sometimes the pattern "sounds right" even when the facts are wrong.

The LLM is trying to be helpful. When it doesn't know something, it may still try to answer instead of admitting, *I'm not sure.*

If an answer seems suspicious, it is okay for you to ask ChatGPT, *Tell me what you are confident about and what you are unsure about.*

#34 Frequently Asked Questions

1. **What exactly is ChatGPT?**

ChatGPT is a computer program that you can talk to in plain English.

You type a question, a request, or even a half-formed thought. ChatGPT answers back in sentences that sound like they came from a person.

It can explain things. It can summarize things. It can help you write. It can brainstorm ideas. It can troubleshoot problems. It can make jokes, draft emails, suggest recipes, explain confusing topics, and help you get unstuck when your brain has gone out for coffee.

The "GPT" part stands for Generative Pre-trained Transformer, which sounds like something from a science fiction movie. You do not need to remember that. The useful part is this:

ChatGPT has read a huge amount of text and learned patterns from it. When you ask a question, it predicts a helpful answer based on those patterns.

That does not mean it is a person. It does not mean it is always right. It does not mean it "knows" things the same way you and I know things.

A simple way to think about it: ChatGPT is like having a very patient assistant who has read a ridiculous number of books, websites, examples, explanations, and conversations — and is willing to help you think through almost anything. But it still needs your guidance.

The better you explain what you want, the better it can help. For example, instead of typing: *Write something about dogs.*

You might type: *Write a funny 200-word story about a golden retriever who thinks he is the mayor of the neighborhood.*

That second request gives ChatGPT a much better target.

So, what exactly is ChatGPT?

It is a conversation partner, writing helper, tutor, brainstorming buddy, translator, explainer, and occasional digital goofball. It is not magic. But some days, it sure feels close.

2. **Is ChatGPT the same thing as artificial intelligence?**

Not exactly. That would be like asking, *Is Excel the same thing as Microsoft Office?*

Excel is one part of Microsoft Office. A very important part, obviously. I would say the best part. But Word, PowerPoint, Outlook, and Teams are also in the family.

ChatGPT is one part of the much bigger world of artificial intelligence, usually shortened to AI.

AI is the broad idea of computers doing tasks that used to require human intelligence. That might include recognizing faces in photos, recommending the next video you should watch, spotting fraud on a credit card, translating a sentence into another language, or helping a car stay in its lane.

ChatGPT is a specific kind of AI called a chatbot. More specifically, it is powered by a large language model, or LLM. That means it is especially good at language.

You can ask it to explain something, rewrite something, brainstorm something, summarize something, or help you think through a problem. It works with words the way Excel works with numbers, formulas, and grids.

So no, ChatGPT is not the same thing as artificial intelligence. ChatGPT is one example of AI. A very useful example. A sometimes amazing example.

And every once in a while, an example that confidently gives you an answer that makes you say, *Buddy, where on earth did you get that?*

3. **Does ChatGPT actually "think" or understand me?**

That depends on what you mean by "think." ChatGPT does not think the way you think. It does not sit there with a cup of coffee, stare out the window, remember third grade, worry about the electric bill, and then decide what to say next.

"Worrying about the electric bill" is funnier after you read "#37 Environmental Issues Surrounding AI" on page 152

It does not have feelings. It does not have beliefs. It does not wake up in the morning hoping today is the day it finally understands VLOOKUP.

But it is very good at something that can look like thinking.

ChatGPT reads your words, looks at the conversation so far, and predicts a useful response. It has learned from a massive amount of text, so it has seen many examples of how people explain ideas, solve problems, tell stories, write emails, argue politely, argue badly, and occasionally use the phrase "circle back" when everyone in the meeting is already dead inside.

So does it "understand" you? In a human sense, no. In a practical sense, often yes.

If you say: *Explain this like I am brand new to computers.* ChatGPT can adjust.

If you say: *Make this sound friendlier but still professional.* ChatGPT can do that.

If you say: *I am frustrated and need help figuring out what to do next.* ChatGPT can respond in a way that feels surprisingly thoughtful.

That does not mean there is a tiny person inside the machine. It means the tool is very good at recognizing patterns in language and producing responses that match what you need.

Here is the way I think about it:

ChatGPT does not understand you like a close friend understands you. But it can understand your instructions well enough to be useful. And for a tool, useful is a pretty good place to start.

4. **Why does ChatGPT sometimes make things up?**

Because ChatGPT is not a truth machine. That sounds harsh, but it is important.

ChatGPT is a language machine. Its job is to create a response that fits the words you typed. Most of the time, that response is useful. Sometimes it is brilliant. And every now and then, it confidently walks into a wall.

When ChatGPT makes something up, people call that a **hallucination**.

I do not love that word, because it makes it sound mysterious and spooky. What is really happening is simpler: ChatGPT is trying to give you a helpful answer, but it does not always know where the facts stop and the guessing begins.

It might invent a book title that sounds real.

It might quote a study that does not exist.

It might give you an Excel function that looks like it should work, but Excel looks at it and says, "Nice try, champ."

It might answer a question about a current event using old information.

It might accept a false idea hidden inside your question. If you ask, *Why did Microsoft remove PivotTables from Excel?* ChatGPT might start explaining the reason, instead of first saying, *Hold on. They did not remove PivotTables.*

This has gotten much better than it was in the early days. Newer versions are better at saying *I'm not sure*, checking sources, using tools, and slowing down before giving an answer. But the problem has not disappeared. The safest way to use ChatGPT is to remember this: **ChatGPT can sound confident even when it is wrong**.

That does not make it useless. Far from it. A calculator can still be useful even if you accidentally type the wrong number. Excel can still be useful even if your formula points to the wrong cell. The tool is powerful, but you still have to bring judgment.

Here are a few ways to reduce made-up answers:

- Ask it to say when it is unsure.
- Ask it to separate facts from guesses.
- Ask it to use sources when facts matter.

Be careful with questions that contain assumptions. Instead of asking: *Why did this company go bankrupt?* Try: *Did this company go bankrupt? Check that first, then explain what happened.*

That one little change can save you from a very polished answer to a question based on nonsense.

ChatGPT is not perfect. But if you treat it like a smart assistant who occasionally needs adult supervision, you will get much better results.

5. **Can I trust the answers ChatGPT gives me?**

Sometimes. How is that for a comforting answer?

Here is the better version: You can often trust ChatGPT to be useful. You should not automatically trust it to be correct. That difference matters.

ChatGPT is great at explaining ideas, rewriting confusing text, brainstorming possibilities, helping you organize your thoughts, and giving you a place to start. It can take a messy paragraph and make it clearer. It can explain a topic five different ways until one of them finally clicks. It can help you write the email you have been avoiding since Tuesday.

But when facts matter, you need to slow down.

If ChatGPT says, *Here is a good way to organize your garage,* you can probably use your judgment and move on with your life.

If ChatGPT says, *Here is how to treat chest pain, Here is what this tax form means*, or *Here is the legal deadline for filing an appeal*, do not just salute and march off a cliff.

For important topics, treat ChatGPT like a smart assistant, not the final authority. Ask follow-up questions:

- How sure are you?
- What are you basing that on?
- What parts should I verify?
- Can you separate confirmed facts from assumptions?
- Can you cite a reliable source?

This is especially important for medical, legal, financial, tax, current events, travel rules, prices, software features, and anything involving "as of today."

ChatGPT can also be wonderfully confident while being wrong. That is the part that gets people in trouble. It will not always mumble, look nervous, and say, *I made that up*. Sometimes it will put on a nice shirt, speak in complete sentences, and hand you nonsense with excellent grammar.

So can you trust it?

- Trust it to help you think.
- Trust it to help you draft.
- Trust it to help you learn.

But when the answer matters, verify.

The best rule is this: Use ChatGPT as a very helpful first draft, not as the last word. That one habit will save you a lot of trouble.

6. **What should I never type into ChatGPT?**

Here is the simple rule: Do not type anything into ChatGPT that you would not want stored, copied, forwarded, leaked, subpoenaed, misunderstood, or accidentally shown on a projector during a meeting.

That sounds dramatic. Good. It should.

ChatGPT can be incredibly useful, but you still need to use common sense. Do not paste your entire life into the box just because the box is friendly and answers quickly.

Avoid entering things like:

- Social Security numbers.
- Bank account numbers.
- Credit card numbers.
- Passwords.
- Private medical records.
- Secret company documents.
- Confidential customer lists.
- Legal documents that you are not allowed to share.
- Anything that would get you fired, sued, divorced, or grounded.

Also be careful with other people's private information. It is one thing to ask: *Help me write a polite email to my doctor asking about this bill.*

It is another thing to paste in a giant medical record with names, birth dates, insurance numbers, and every detail since 1997. When possible, remove the private details first.

Instead of: *My employee Jane Smith, Social Security number 123-45-6789, is having payroll trouble...*

Try: *An employee is having payroll trouble. Help me write a note to HR. Do not include private details.*

You can still get plenty of help without handing over the keys to the kingdom.

For work, follow your company's rules. Some companies allow AI tools. Some ban them. Some provide a special business version that protects company data better than a regular public chatbot. Use the approved tool, not whatever you found at midnight while eating cereal over the sink.

For personal use, be smart. ChatGPT does not need your password to help you write a better password policy.

It does not need your bank account number to explain compound interest.

It does not need your full medical chart to help you prepare questions for your doctor.

When in doubt, anonymize.

Change names. Remove account numbers. Delete addresses. Replace private details with placeholders like `[customer name]`, `[account number]`, or `[diagnosis]`.

The goal is not to be paranoid. The goal is to be careful.

ChatGPT is a helpful assistant. Do not treat it like a locked diary.

7. **Does ChatGPT remember what I tell it?**

Sometimes.

That answer is annoying. But it is the honest one.

ChatGPT has a few different kinds of "memory," and they do not all work the same way.

First, ChatGPT can remember what you said earlier in the same conversation. If you say: *Explain this like I am ten years old.* And then, three messages later, you say: *Now give me an example.*

ChatGPT usually knows that you still want the ten-year-old version. It is using the current conversation as context.

That is the easy kind of memory.

The second kind is saved memory. If memory is turned on, ChatGPT may remember useful things about you for future chats. For example, it might remember that you prefer short answers, that you are learning Spanish, or that your dog is named Waffles and believes the sofa belongs to him.

That can be handy. You do not have to keep repeating yourself every time.

There is also a setting that can let ChatGPT refer back to past conversations. That means a new chat may be able to use useful details from older chats, not because the same little robot has been sitting there waiting for you, but because the system can pull in relevant context.

This is powerful.

It is also why you should be thoughtful about what you type.

You are not helpless, though. You can ask ChatGPT: What do you remember about me?

You can also ask it to forget something. And in settings, you can turn memory features on or off.

If you want a conversation that does not use or create memories, look for a dotted Temporary Chat icon in the top right of a new chat window. That is the *let's not write this in the notebook* option. In August 2026, OpenAI announced a "personalized temporary chat". This chat would not get saved but could refer to existing memories or custom instructions.

One more important point:

Deleting a memory and deleting a chat are not always the same thing. If ChatGPT remembered a detail from a conversation, you may need to manage the memory and the chat history separately.

So, does ChatGPT remember what you tell it? In the same chat, usually yes. Across different chats, maybe, depending on your settings.

Forever, perfectly, and exactly like a human friend? No.

Think of ChatGPT memory as a helpful notebook, not a sacred vault.

Useful? Yes. Convenient? Absolutely. Something you should understand before typing in your deepest secrets, company strategy, or Aunt Linda's potato salad scandal? Also yes.

8. **What is the difference between a short prompt and a good prompt?**

A short prompt is not always bad.

A good prompt is not always long.

That is the first thing to know.

You can type: *Explain photosynthesis.* That is short. And ChatGPT will probably give you a decent answer.

But if you type: *Explain photosynthesis in plain English for a curious adult who has not taken a science class in 30 years. Use a simple analogy and keep it under 300 words.*

Now ChatGPT has a target. That is the difference.

A short prompt says: *Do something.*

A good prompt says: *Do this specific thing, for this audience, in this style, with these limits.*

Think of it like asking someone to make dinner. If you say: *Make food.* Well, congratulations. You might get soup, tacos, oatmeal, or a suspicious casserole from the back of the freezer.

If you say: *Make a quick dinner for four people, no bell peppers, not too spicy, and use the chicken we already have in the fridge.* Now we are getting somewhere.

ChatGPT works the same way.

A good prompt usually includes a few helpful details:

- What do you want?
- Who is it for?
- What style should it use?
- How long should it be?
- What should it avoid?
- What information should it use?

For example, instead of: Write an *email.*

Try: *Write a friendly but professional email to a customer explaining that the shipment is delayed by two days. Apologize, do not blame the warehouse, and offer to update them tomorrow.*

That is not fancy. That is not "prompt engineering." That is just giving decent instructions. You do not have to learn magic words. You do not have to chant in binary. You do not have to say, *Act as a world-class productivity ninja with 40 years of cross-functional thought leadership.* Please don't, actually.

Just tell ChatGPT what you are trying to do.

A good prompt is clear, specific, and honest about the goal.

And here is the best part: your first prompt does not have to be perfect. You can start short: *Help me plan a birthday toast.*

Then improve it: *Make it funny, warm, and under two minutes. Mention that she loves gardening, hates being the center of attention, and once rescued a cake from falling off a table.*

That back-and-forth is where ChatGPT gets really useful.

So the difference is not short versus long. The difference is vague versus clear. Short can work. Clear works better.

9. **Can ChatGPT help with work, school, hobbies, and everyday life?**

Yes.

That is one of the best things about ChatGPT. It is not just for computer programmers, tech billionaires, or people who say "synergy" without laughing.

ChatGPT can help with ordinary life.

At work, it can help you write emails, summarize meetings, brainstorm ideas, clean up confusing instructions, prepare for presentations, draft reports, and figure out why the spreadsheet you inherited appears to have been built by raccoons.

At school, it can explain difficult topics, help you study, create practice quizzes, review your writing, suggest outlines, and explain the same idea three different ways until one finally makes sense.

For hobbies, it can help you plan a garden, learn guitar chords, write a short story, organize a trip, identify what kind of bird keeps yelling at you, or figure out why your sourdough starter looks like a science experiment with abandonment issues.

For everyday life, it can help with meal ideas, polite text messages, birthday toasts, travel plans, repair questions, shopping comparisons, checklists, routines, and those little life problems that are too small for a professional but too annoying to ignore.

Here is the trick: Do not wait for a "big enough" problem. ChatGPT is often most useful for the small stuff.

Try:

- *Help me write a nicer version of this message.*
- *Explain this bill in plain English.*
- *Give me five dinner ideas using chicken, rice, and whatever dignity I have left.*
- *Help me make a packing list for a three-day trip.*
- *Quiz me on this chapter.*
- *Turn these messy notes into a clear plan.*
- *Help me think through the pros and cons.*

That last one is important. ChatGPT is not just an answer machine. It is also a thinking partner. You can use it when you are stuck, tired, overwhelmed, curious, bored, or staring at a blank page like it personally insulted you.

Can it help with work, school, hobbies, and everyday life? Absolutely.

Just remember: it helps best when you give it a real job to do.

Not: *Help.*

Try: *I am overwhelmed by this project. Ask me three questions, then help me make a simple next-step plan.*

That is when ChatGPT starts to feel less like a search box and more like a patient assistant who does not judge you for needing help finding the thing that is already in your hand.

10. **What changes if I pay for ChatGPT Plus?**

The free version of ChatGPT is a little like walking into Costco for the free samples. You can absolutely get something useful.

But if you start using ChatGPT every day, sooner or later you may want the bigger cart. That is where ChatGPT Plus comes in.

ChatGPT Plus is the paid version for individual users. It gives you more access to the stronger models, higher usage limits, more room for uploads, better access to image creation, deeper research tools, custom GPTs, projects, tasks, and earlier access to some new features.

In plain English: you can do more before ChatGPT taps you on the shoulder and says, *That's enough for now, friend.*

This matters more than beginners expect.

With the free version, you might ask a few questions, get some help, and be perfectly happy. But if you start using ChatGPT to write, learn, plan, analyze files, create images, compare options, summarize documents, or work through a messy project, the limits can show up.

Plus does not make ChatGPT perfect. It does not mean every answer is correct. It does not mean you can stop thinking, checking, or using common sense. But it usually gives you more power and fewer interruptions.

Here are the kinds of things Plus can help with:

- You can ask more questions before hitting limits.
- You can use more advanced models more often.
- You can upload files and ask questions about them.
- You can create and edit images with more room to work.
- You can use tools for research, projects, tasks, and custom GPTs.
- You may get new features earlier than free users.

For a casual user, the free plan may be enough. If you only ask ChatGPT one question every few days, do not rush to hand over your credit card like it is a Black Friday pizza oven.

But if ChatGPT starts becoming part of your daily routine, Plus can feel like the difference between borrowing a bicycle and owning a pickup truck. The bicycle is fine. The pickup truck lets you haul a refrigerator.

My advice? Start free. Use it for real things.

When you find yourself saying, *I wish I could do more of this*, then Plus starts to make sense.

Do not upgrade because you are curious. Upgrade because you have found a use for it.

11. **Will AI replace me?**

Maybe.

Well, that got dark fast.

Here is the more useful answer: AI probably will not replace *you.*

But someone who knows how to use AI may replace someone who refuses to learn it.

That does not mean you need to become a programmer, data scientist, robot mechanic, or the person in the meeting who says "large language model" eleven times before lunch.

It means you should learn enough to use the tool.

Think about what happened with spreadsheets.

When Excel showed up, it changed office work forever. It did not eliminate accountants, analysts, bookkeepers, managers, teachers, and small business owners. But it absolutely changed what good work looked like.

The person with a calculator and a green ledger book could still be smart. But the person who learned Excel could do more, faster.

AI feels similar. It can write a rough draft. It can summarize a long document. It can explain confusing ideas. It can brainstorm twenty options when your brain has exactly zero. It can help you learn, laugh, and get unstuck.

But it still needs a human in the loop. It needs someone to ask the right question. It needs someone to know whether the answer makes sense.

It needs someone to bring taste, judgment, experience, values, humor, courage, and context.

That is you.

AI can generate a sympathy note. It cannot actually care about your friend.

AI can suggest a business idea. It cannot know what kind of life you want to build.

AI can draft a wedding toast. It cannot remember when your sister fell into the lake at age nine and came out yelling that she meant to do that.

The danger is not that AI becomes you.

The danger is that you ignore AI until other people are using it to move faster, learn faster, write better, make better decisions, and solve problems with a bigger toolbox.

So will AI replace you? Not if you treat it like a tool worth learning.

The goal is not to compete against AI. The goal is to become the person who knows how to use AI well.

You plus AI is the interesting part. You without AI may still be fine. But you plus AI gets a really nice head start.

#35 AI Glossary

If you start discussing AI with others, you will hear a lot of jargon. Here is a glossary of terms, organized by theme:

The Basics

AI / Artificial Intelligence: The broad idea of computers doing tasks that seem smart.

Chatbot: A program you can talk with by typing or speaking.

ChatGPT: A chatbot made by OpenAI that can answer questions, write, explain, brainstorm, and help with many everyday tasks.

LLM / Large Language Model: The kind of AI behind ChatGPT. It works with language and predicts helpful responses based on patterns.

Model: The AI engine behind the chatbot. Different models may be faster, smarter, cheaper, or better at different tasks.

Mumbling: The brief phrases that appear before a chatbot begins working on your prompt. They often describe what the chatbot plans to do and disappear once the actual response begins.

Prompt: The question or instruction you type into ChatGPT.

Response: The answer ChatGPT gives back.

How to ask better questions

Context: The information ChatGPT is using right now, including your prompt, earlier parts of the conversation, and sometimes files or memories.

Context Window: The amount of recent conversation, instructions, and uploaded information ChatGPT can "see" while answering you. If you continue a chat for many days, the context window can get too large and the responses may seem confused. It is time to start a new chat.

Example Prompt: A sample question or instruction that shows ChatGPT the kind of answer, format, or style you want.

Token Limit: The maximum amount of text ChatGPT can handle at one time, including your prompt, the conversation, files, and its answer.

Two Kinds of Computing

CPU Computing: Traditional computing that process explicit hard-coded instructions to process data.

LLMs:- use neural networks to reason based on probability.

Why answers can be wrong

Hallucination: When ChatGPT gives an answer that sounds confident but is wrong or made up.

Temperature: A setting that controls how predictable or creative an AI's answers are. Ranges from 0.0 to 1.0. A low setting such as 0.0 to 0.3 makes the answers more predictable. A higher temperature can lead to creative, diverse, or unpredictable answers.

Non-deterministic: Give an LLM the same question multiple times and you will get different answers. This is the opposite of Probabilistic - where everytime you enter =LEN("Strawberry") into Excel, you will get an answer of 10.

Personalization and privacy

Memory: Information ChatGPT may save and use in future chats, depending on your settings.

Temporary Chat: A chat mode meant for conversations you do not want saved or remembered. To start a temporary chat, open the Model drop-down at the top of ChatGPT. Choose Temporary Chat.

Privacy: What happens to the information you type, upload, or ask ChatGPT to remember.

Things ChatGPT can do

Upload: Giving ChatGPT a file, image, PDF, spreadsheet, or document to work with.

Voice Mode: Talking to ChatGPT out loud instead of typing.

Image Generation: Asking ChatGPT to create a picture from your description.

Deep Research: A tool that can spend more effort researching a topic and summarizing what it finds.

Custom GPT: A customized version of ChatGPT built for a specific purpose, like helping with recipes, tutoring, or analyzing documents. Bill Jelen is likely to insert an ad near the end of this book for his book on Custom GPT.

Agent: AI that can take steps toward a goal, often using tools.

Want to Keep Learning?

One of my favorite ways to keep up with AI is the **UW-Stout Polytechnic Weekly AI Meetup**, hosted by Emily Laird at the University of Wisconsin-Stout Polytechnic.

It is a friendly weekly Zoom discussion where beginners, educators, business people, and AI nerds can hear what is changing, ask questions, and learn the vocabulary that keeps showing up in the AI world. Search for UW-Stout AI Weekly Meetup page for information on how to join.

Here are a few advanced terms you may hear there.

API: ChatGPT offers a paid Application Programming Interface where other software can call ChatGPT.

Embedding: A numerical fingerprint of text, images, or other information that helps AI compare meanings instead of just matching exact words.

Fine-tuning: Training an existing AI model further so it becomes better at a specific style, task, or subject area.

Guardrails: Rules, filters, and safety instructions that try to keep an AI system from giving harmful, private, or wildly inappropriate answers.

Pre-Training: The early training stage where an AI model learns broad patterns from huge amounts of text, code, images, or other data before it is customized for specific uses.

Post-Training: The later training stage where an AI model is adjusted to be more helpful, safer, more accurate, and better at following human instructions.

RAG / Retrieval-Augmented Generation: A method where AI first retrieves relevant information from documents or databases, then uses that information to answer your question.

Token A small chunk of text that an AI model reads or writes, roughly like a piece of a word. If you move on to business subscriptions to LLMs, you might find yourself paying by the token.

Transformer The AI architecture behind many modern language models, designed to pay attention to relationships between words and ideas.

Vector database A special database that stores embeddings so AI can quickly find information with similar meaning. My favorite Vector explanation is from AI author Rob Collie: If you combine the vector for the word "hot" with the vector for the word "dog", you will end up with a vector close to the word "sausage". This is how the LLM figures out that you are talking about a hot dog sandwich instead of a sheepdog at the equator.

Agentic Workflows Multi-step AI processes where the AI plans, uses tools, checks results, and continues working toward a goal.

MCP / Model Context Protocol A standard way for AI systems to connect with outside tools, files, services, and data sources.

Skills Think of skills as special tools in the AI's toolbox. Some examples include writing Python code, reading a spreadsheet, searching the web, creating an image, summarizing a PDF, or following a special writing style.

System Prompts Behind-the-scenes instructions that guide how an AI behaves before the user types anything.

Zero-Shot Prompting Asking AI to do a task without giving it an example first.

Few-Shot Prompting Giving AI one or more examples so it can imitate the pattern you want.

GDP-Val A benchmark that tests how well AI models perform on real-world work tasks across many occupations. When a new LLM model is announced, the first thing I do is check how it scored on GDP-Val. As this book is being written, the best GDP-Val score in August of 2026 is Claude Opus 5 with a score of 1860. Just 18 months ago, the best models were scoring in the 800's.

Local AI AI that runs on your own computer or device instead of sending every request to a cloud service. Popular with people concerned about privacy. Note that the open-source models available for Local AI are generally about a year behind commercial models.

People

You will routinely hear about these people and companies at the UW-Stout AI Meetup:

Sam Altman: Founder of OpenAI, the Creator of ChatGPT

Dario and Daniela Amodei: Founders of Anthropic. Dario and his sister Daniela left OpenAI in 2021 due to directional differences regarding AI safety.

Elon Musk: Founder of Grok

Jensen Huang: CEO of NVIDIA. NVIDIA is a chip maker who is leading the AI race. Their GPUs are uniquely designed to perform thousands of tasks simultaneously.

Satya Nadella: CEO of Microsoft. Famously orchestrated Microsoft's multi-billion dollar partnership with OpenAI.

#36 What Would Oliver Remington Do?

I had the chance to talk with Florida artist Ollie Remington for several hours one day in 2013. He is an interesting guy. Before becoming an artist, he was a salesman for the Fort Pierce Typewriter Company.

Let that sink in for a minute. Here is a guy, making a great living selling typerwriters up and down the east coast of Florida.

When I met him, he was working under a pop-up tent in his driveway, making four original paintings a day. He was hoping that crazy people like me would somehow show up at his door.

I think back and wonder, when the typewriter salesman first heard about a word processor, how did he react? With fear? With anger? It is not a perfect comparison, because the shift took ten years and reached a tipping point in 1984. But me, as a Monday-Morning Quarterback some 40 years later, I am screaming back through time telling Ollie that he should embrace technology and learn about Word Processors.

For me, I've decided to lean in and embrace AI. If we have something that makes the MrExcel Message Board obsolete, let me learn about it and find a way that I can be useful in the AI economy.

#37 Environmental Issues Surrounding AI

AI feels weightless because it appears as text on a screen, but behind it are data centers, electricity demand, cooling systems, water use, chips, rare-earth mining, backup generators, and grid strain. For people already worried about climate change, drought, and corporate overconsumption, AI can look like a luxury technology burning real-world resources to produce LinkedIn posts, fake images, spam, and chatbot answers.

Water use is the most visible local issue

AI data centers generate enormous heat, and many facilities use evaporative cooling, which consumes freshwater. Some large data centers can use millions of gallons per day, roughly comparable to the water use of a small town. The concern gets sharper when these centers are built in drought-prone places or fast-growing regions already fighting over water.

The tradeoff is ugly: save water or save electricity

Evaporative cooling uses water but can reduce electricity demand. Air cooling uses less water but may require more power, especially in hot climates. So the "green" answer depends on location, grid mix, weather, and whether the water is potable, recycled, reclaimed, or drawn from stressed sources.

> Gwen recently told me that https://ecogpt.com/ is an company that plants trees to offset the impact of using them.

Electricity demand is the bigger global issue

The International Energy Association (IEA) says AI is accelerating the buildout of high-performance servers, and data-center electricity demand is now a major planning issue for power grids. More AI means more GPUs, more cooling, more transmission, and in some regions more fossil-fuel generation to meet peak demand.

The local community often sees the downside first

A data center may bring tax revenue and some jobs, but residents may see water withdrawals, the hum of noisy backup generators, power-grid strain, higher electric rates, land use, and big industrial buildings. That is why opposition is rising around proposed data centers. Google's 2024 data centers used 7.2 billion gallons of freshwater and replenished about 64%, which helps explain why water has become a public-relations and permitting issue.

AI companies argue the per-prompt footprint is small

Google researchers reported that the median Gemini Apps text prompt used about 0.24 Wh of energy and about 0.26 mL of water, which is tiny at the individual-prompt level. But critics respond: multiply tiny by billions of prompts, model training, data-center construction, chip manufacturing, and idle capacity, and it becomes a real infrastructure footprint.

There are better cooling designs, but they are unevenly deployed. Closed-loop liquid cooling can dramatically reduce direct water consumption. Microsoft recently said some new AI data centers will use closed-loop systems that consume very little new water during normal operation, but many existing facilities still rely on older methods.

The environmental bottom line

AI is not automatically an environmental disaster per question asked. But the AI boom is driving a massive buildout of energy-hungry, heat-producing infrastructure, and the environmental costs are local, uneven, and often hidden.

That becomes a very legitimate reason for rebellion: people feel they are being asked to accept water use, power-grid strain, and carbon emissions so that companies can generate more chatbots, ads, slop content, and automated middle management.

#38 Social Issues Surrounding AI

A lot of people are negative about AI. Particularly young adults. As your enthusiasm for AI grows, you might run into people who have different feelings than yours about AI.

It is best to know the issues so you can make an informed decision. I read this list. I've already watched AI remove my place in the workforce. I am still embracing it, because I don't see any way to stop it.

Fear of job loss and entry-level career collapse

For students, artists, writers, coders, designers, analysts, and entry-level workers, AI looks like a machine aimed directly at the first rung of the career ladder. One teen survey found 57% believed AI had negatively affected their career outlook, and a Harvard Youth Poll report said 59% of 18–29-year-olds viewed AI as a threat to job prospects.

Creative work being scraped, copied, and devalued

A lot of generative AI was trained on writing, art, code, music, and images scraped from the web. Artists especially object because the machine can imitate a style, undercut rates, and erase credit. A 2026 survey of verified professional visual artists found most were strongly opposed to generative AI and reported stress plus reduced job opportunities

Loss of trust: hallucinations, deepfakes, fake content

People see hallucinations, fake citations, deepfakes, biased answers, AI slop, fake images, spam content, and automated customer service hell. Pew found U.S. adults are much more likely to feel concerned than excited about AI in daily life: 50% concerned versus 10% excited. The other 40% are equally concerned and excited.

Power concentration by big tech companies

The winners appear to be giant tech companies with data centers, chips, copyrighted training data, and legal teams. The losers appear to be freelancers, junior employees, teachers, artists, and small publishers. That makes AI feel less like "democratized creativity" and more like another wealth transfer upward.

AI being forced into work, school, and software without consent

A lot of AI adoption is top-down: companies add AI, schools scramble, platforms inject AI buttons everywhere. People rebel when they feel they never consented to the change.

Fear of becoming dependent or mentally lazy

The fear is not just "AI will replace me." It is "AI will make me mentally flabby." Research on AI-assisted writing suggests the outcome depends heavily on how people use it: active exploration can help, but mindless editing/copying can reduce idea development.

Human identity and meaning being cheapened

Young people spend years learning to write, draw, compose, code, or think clearly. Then someone types "make it better" and gets a plausible result in ten seconds. Even when the AI output is mediocre, the emotional message is brutal: "Your hard-earned skill is now a button."

#39 This Has Happened Before

But not exactly like this.

Whenever a powerful new technology arrives, the first wave of reaction is rarely calm. People do not look at a typewriter, a spreadsheet, a web browser, a smartphone, Netflix, or ChatGPT and immediately say, "Ah yes, a balanced tool with tradeoffs." They say, "What is this going to destroy?"

That is not a foolish question.

Oliver Remington, selling typewriters in Fort Pierce, probably did not wake up one morning and declare himself obsolete. He had customers. He had a product people understood. He had a business model. Then computers arrived. Word processors arrived. Printers arrived. The world did not hold a vote. It simply moved.

That is the uncomfortable part of technological change: it does not wait for permission from the people whose lives it rearranges.

The spreadsheet revolution changed accounting and management. Suddenly, one person with VisiCalc or Lotus 1-2-3 could model things that previously required a department. The web revolution changed publishing, retail, research, advertising, and how people found answers. Mobile phones changed where the internet lived; it moved from the desk to the pocket. Streaming services changed entertainment and helped push DVDs from everyday objects to attic clutter. They also created a new kind of invisible infrastructure problem: millions of people watching high-definition video at the same time, expecting the internet to simply handle it.

Now AI has arrived, and it touches even more sensitive territory.

AI is not merely replacing a device or changing where we buy things. It seems to reach into writing, drawing, coding, teaching, analyzing, summarizing, composing, researching, and decision-making. It raises environmental questions about electricity, water, chips, and data centers. It raises social questions about jobs, creativity, fairness, trust, education, privacy, and who gets to profit from the work of millions of humans.

So yes, the fear is real. But fear has been present at every major shift.

The useful question is not, "Were the doomsayers wrong?"

The useful question is, "What were they right about, what did they miss, and what should we do differently this time?"

The summary below looks back at several major technology shifts that happened during my lifetime: computing before the internet, spreadsheets, the web, streaming, mobile, and AI.

In each case, people worried that something human, valuable, or stable was about to be lost. Sometimes they exaggerated. Sometimes they nailed it. And sometimes the technology created new opportunities that were impossible to see from the doorway of the old world.

Oliver Remington reminds us to ask the human question first: not "Can this new thing win?" but "What happens to the people standing in its path?"

Computing before the internet

Doomsayers: "Computers will destroy clerical jobs, dehumanize work, centralize control, and make people dependent on machines."

Reality: Computers did eliminate many repetitive clerical tasks and changed the skills workers needed. But they also made calculations faster, improved recordkeeping, reduced errors, helped scientists and engineers solve previously impossible problems, and gave businesses tools that had once been available only to large institutions. Entire industries grew around software, hardware, data processing, and technical support. The fears about job loss, inequality, and dehumanization were real, but so were the enormous gains in productivity, discovery, and access to information.

Spreadsheet revolution

Doomsayers: "Managers will build bad models, accountants will make invisible errors, people will trust numbers they don't understand, and finance will become reckless."

Reality: All true sometimes! But spreadsheets also became the killer app for personal computing. VisiCalc helped turn the Apple II from hobbyist toy into a business machine. People who excelled at spreadsheets saw their value at work increase for 30+ years.

Web revolution

Doomsayers: "The web will destroy newspapers, retail stores, privacy, attention spans, and trusted information."

Reality: Also partly true. The web gutted classifieds and transformed journalism, but it also created e-commerce, search, blogs, forums, social media, and instant access to information. Even Microsoft initially underestimated how thoroughly the web could shift computing away from the Windows desktop. It quickly changed course, launching Internet Explorer and rebuilding much of its strategy around the internet.

Video Streaming

Doomsayers: Streaming will kill DVDs, video stores, cable TV, movie theaters, and shared cultural moments. It will overwhelm internet bandwidth, make entertainment disposable, and turn every company into a subscription tollbooth.

Reality: DVDs and video stores collapsed, cable weakened. Movie theaters stuggled but survived. Internet traffic surged. But streaming also gave viewers instant access, created new original programming, rescued niche content, and changed expectations forever: people now assume any movie, show, clip, tutorial, or live event should be available on demand, on any device.

Mobile revolution

Doomsayers: "Phones will make us distracted, addicted, rude, tracked, anxious, and always working."

Reality: Again: annoyingly accurate in places. Smartphones became nearly universal. Pew says about 91% of U.S. adults now own one. But the concerns about attention, teen mental health, privacy, and constant availability never went away.

AI revolution

Doomsayers: AI will take jobs, steal creative work, flood the world with fake content, weaken learning, concentrate power, consume energy and water, and make humans feel less necessary.

Reality: Too early to score. But the fear is sharper because AI touches cognition itself: writing, coding, summarizing, teaching, designing, deciding. It does not just automate a task; it appears to automate judgment.

So What Would Oliver Remington Do?

Looking back at these revolutions, one pattern is hard to miss: the doomsayers were never completely wrong.

Computers did eliminate some jobs. Spreadsheets did create dangerous errors. The web did damage newspapers, retail, and privacy. Streaming did weaken DVDs, video stores, and cable. Mobile did make us distracted and always reachable. AI will change jobs, creativity, education, publishing, software, and the way people think about expertise.

The mistake is not in worrying. The mistake is in stopping there.

Oliver Remington could have spent the rest of his life yelling at word processors. He could have made a perfectly reasonable case that typewriters were honest machines. They did not crash. They did not need software updates. They did not connect to the internet. They did not ask you to accept a license agreement. A typewriter did one thing, and it did that thing faithfully.

He would not have been wrong. But he also would not have changed the outcome.

The world moved from typewriters to computers because people wanted the new capability. They wanted to revise without retyping the whole page. They wanted to save documents, print clean copies, run spell check, and eventually send those words anywhere in the world. The old tool had virtues. The new tool had leverage.

That is the uncomfortable lesson of every technology shift in this chapter. The new thing is almost never morally pure. It solves problems and creates problems. It removes friction and removes jobs. It gives ordinary people new power and gives large companies even more power. It makes some things easier, some things worse, and some things impossible to put back the way they were.

AI is no different.

Actually, AI may be more personal because it does not merely change how we type, calculate, shop, watch, or communicate. It touches the work many people thought made them special: writing, teaching, coding, designing, analyzing, explaining, creating, and deciding.

That is why the resistance matters. The people raising concerns about AI are not simply afraid of the future. They are asking legitimate questions.

- Who owns the work that trained these systems?
- Who benefits when entry-level jobs disappear?
- Who pays the environmental cost of the data centers?
- Who should regulate AI companies, and how can rules protect people without stopping useful innovation?
- Who decides when AI is good enough to replace a human?
- Who is accountable when AI is wrong?
- And most important: what happens to people whose value was built around skills that machines can now imitate?

Those questions deserve better than a dismissive "adapt or die."

But they also deserve better than pretending AI will go away.

The practical path is somewhere between blind enthusiasm and frozen resistance. Use the tool. Question the tool. Learn its strengths. Notice its failures. Protect human judgment. Teach people how it works. Demand transparency. Push for reasonable limits. Refuse to confuse faster with better. Refuse to confuse cheaper with wiser.

And then ask the Oliver Remington question:

What would a decent, practical, clear-eyed person do when the world changes under his feet?

They would not worship the new machine.

They would not pretend the old world was coming back.

They would learn enough to understand what had changed. They would help other people make sense of it. They would keep the human relationship at the center. And they would look for the place where his experience still mattered.

That is where we are with AI.

This book is not asking you to love AI. It is not asking you to trust it blindly, excuse its costs, or ignore the people harmed by it. It is asking you to understand it well enough that you can make better choices than fear alone would allow.

Because every major shift creates two groups of people: those who are changed by it without understanding it, and those who learn enough to have a say in what happens next.

Be in the second group.

#40 Index